The Back Stories of History

Featuring Arcola

Priscilla T Graham

In the making of this book, every attempt has been made to verify names, facts, and figures. Sources: Texas Historical Association, National Register for Historic Places, Texas Historical Commission Markers, findagrave.com, ancestry.com, fold3.com, Houston Post Newspaper, Church Cornerstones, and Dedication Markers

Photos from the Graham Collection, Richard *Pete* Simon, Mary Etta Anderson, Trinidad Elisa Sanchez, Veeda Williams, and Public Domain (Images available on the Internet and included in accordance with Title 17 U.S.C. Section 107). Cover photo of Major Williams courtesy of Veeda Williams.

Written by Priscilla T Graham
priscillatgraham.com@gmail.com

Cover Design and layout by Priscilla T Graham

Dedicated to the men and women of Arcola!
Black History is American History.

Foreword

BY VEEDA V. WILLIAMS, PHD

I grew up in the small community of Arcola, Texas. The memories made, lessons learned, and values instilled as a result of my rearing, have long been a source of pride which I revisit often.

This work by Priscilla T Graham represents the most comprehensive collection of facts and artifacts referencing the historical documentation of Arcola. As one of the most overlooked cities situated within the fast-paced growth of Fort Bend County, Texas, Arcola has finally begun to experience the growth of new development; thus, the chronicling of its rich history is not only timely, but necessary to forever preserve the significant cultural contexts from which the city emerged.

The Back Stories of History featuring Arcola provides a clear depiction of the places, the people, and the events that shaped the early years of our community It takes us on a journey from the early settlements of the city, beginning in the 1800s, all the way to its present day. Ms. Graham has done an excellent job of amplifying for readers the story of our history and its enduring legacy of survival even in the face of lacking so many resources necessary for any city to thrive.

If one takes only a surface look at the artifacts within the book, from the lens of purely early aesthetics, it may appear there's not much worthy of preserving. However, this *Back Story* has proven to be fertile ground for this long awaited, rich historical accounting of Arcola, Texas; and it is worth the wait.

Content

History of Early Settlement in Fort Bend
Pre-Colonial Inhabitants

Indians inhabited Fort Bend County long before European colonization, living in the region for thousands of years before the arrival of Spanish explorers in the 16th and 17th centuries. The Karankawa and Apache tribes, among others, had established their cultures and ways of life well before Spanish colonization began in the late 1600s.

These tribes had diverse cultures and ways of life, ranging from agricultural societies to nomadic hunters and gatherers. The Karankawa were known for their nomadic lifestyle, relying on fishing and hunting along the Gulf Coast, while the Apache moved frequently in search of resources and often engaged in trade with other tribes.

By 1822, before the first known Anglo settlers arrived in Fort Bend, Texas, the area was home to these Indian tribes who had long been shaping the landscape with their rich and varied cultures.

Anglo Settlers Arrival

However, when Anglo settlers arrived, these tribes faced significant challenges, including devastating epidemics of new diseases like smallpox and measles, which drastically reduced their populations. Additionally, settlers encroached on their lands, leading to conflicts and displacement. The tribes' traditional ways of life were disrupted, and they were often forced into treaties that favored Anglo's interests. Over time, many Indians were either assimilated into Anglo settlers' culture or moved to reservations, resulting in the loss of their cultural heritage and autonomy. These rich and varied cultures laid the foundation for the region's history before the arrival of settlers, and the impact of colonization brought profound changes to their societies.

Transition of Power and Land Grants

The Spanish government controlled the land from the 1600s through the early 1800s. In January 1821, the Spanish government authorized Moses Austin to settle three hundred families in the Brazos and Colorado Rivers valleys. However, Moses Austin died on June 10, 1821, and Mexico declared independence from Spain on August 24, 1821. This period of transition caused delays in Anglo settlers' colonization efforts westward.

Stephen F. Austin and Anglo Settlers Colonization

The newly established Mexican Government approved the Spanish land grants for Anglo Settlers colonization expansion westward in 1823, authorizing Moses Austin's son, Stephen Fuller Austin, to settle three hundred families, known as Austin's Old Three Hundred. Under the empresario contract, Austin granted 297 titles covering 307 parcels of land in Mexican Texas. The Mexican Government issued settlers official documents granting 272 leagues of land in 1824 and 25 leagues of land in 1827.

By 1825, sixty-nine settlers owned 443 enslaved people, comprising a quarter of the colony's population of 1,790. Over the next several years, Austin attained three additional contracts, settling nine hundred more families in the colony, plus an additional eight hundred in partnership with Samuel Williams (Texas State Library Archives, December 5, 2017). In total, 1,540 titles were issued under Austin's leadership. For Anglo settlers to settle in Texas, settlers had to become Mexican citizens and embrace Roman Catholicism.

Original Map
Rosenberg Library
Galveston Tex

David Fitzgerald

David Fitzgerald, his son John, James Frazier, and two enslaved individuals, a man and a woman, escaped from Mississippi to Texas to seek refuge from prosecution. In January 1822, they paddled a canoe up the Brazos de Dios River in search of Stephen F. Austin's colony. They settled on the east bank of the Brazos River, three miles below the present site of Richmond. However, this land was allocated to William Morton. On July 10, 1824, David Fitzgerald, one of Austin's Old Three Hundred, was awarded a league of land (4,428 acres) nineteen miles away in an area known as Long Reach.

Fitzgerald later traded a quarter league of land with Morton, which matched the amount he had claimed from Morton's grant three miles downstream from Fort Bend. Morton's daughter, Louisa Morton, who married Daniel Perry, later inherited the exchanged quarter league.

10

Early Settlement in Long Reach

The first individuals to inhabit Fitzgerald's tract of land in Long Reach were a Black man and a German named John McCloskey. Before Fitzgerald could officially claim the land, it needed to be cleared, and crops had to be planted. Fitzgerald left the men in Long Reach to clear the land and plant corn (Sowell, A.J., 1904, pg. 88).

After Fitzgerald died in 1832, his daughter, Sarah Catherine Fitzgerald, and her husband, Eli Fenn, inherited a portion of her father's property. Sarah and Eli had two sons, John Rutherford and Jesse T. Fenn. John Fitzgerald, Jr., deeded his inheritance of his father's property in the Northwest quarter of the David Fitzgerald league to his sister Sarah Fitzgerald Fenn for $100 on May 12, 1838. John was later elected justice of the peace of the 8th District of Harris County on February 4, 1839. Sarah's husband, Eli Fenn, died in 1840 and was buried on the bank of the Brazos River on the David Fitzgerald League. Sarah remarried Collin Cox shortly after Eli's death.

On November 23, 1840, in the Republic of Texas, Sarah Fitzgerald Cox sold 625 acres of land to Robert G. Waters for $3,125. *Beginning on the east bank of the Brazos River at the southwest corner of the northwest quarter of a League of land granted originally to David Fitzgerald, the land continued with distances given in varas and degrees and markings of X or W placed on trees—toothache tree, hackberry 8 inches in diameter, pecan 3 feet in diameter—crossing Oyster Creek twice, stakes in the ground, more varas and degrees, a 6-inch wild China tree, then back to a stake on the river thence down the river with the meandering thereof to the place of beginning* (Fenn, Mona Moyle, Glimpses of Our History, 2003).

Arcola Sugar Plantation

Robert G. Waters' uncle, Johnathon Dawson Waters, and his friends went to Cox's home and murdered him in front of his wife, Sarah Fitzgerald Cox, over a land dispute. Johnathon Dawson Waters arrived in Texas on March 1, 1840, purchasing a large plantation and naming it Arcola. He purchased his nephew's property along with many surrounding lands, including sections of the Moses Shipman, Thomas Barnett, William Hall, Francis Bingham, and William Pettus leagues (Bones, Francis, 1968). This acquisition led to the creation of one of the largest sugar cane and cotton plantations in Texas, known as the Arcola Sugar Plantation on Oyster Creek.

Waters named his plantation Arcola, drawing inspiration from the picturesque Town of Arcola in Italy. Despite having no personal or familial ties to Italy, the name reflected his vision of creating a grand and prosperous estate. The plantation, often referred to as "her," was personified as a nurturing and sustaining entity, symbolizing the deep connection and dependence people had on the land and its productivity. This practice of personifying land and properties was common during the mid-19th century, particularly from the 1840s to the 1870s, especially in southern states like Texas. Settlers and landowners frequently named their estates after significant places or sources of inspiration, reflecting the era's appreciation for the nurturing qualities of the land.

In 1849, Waters constructed two sugar mills, a brickyard, a sawmill, a sugar barn, a cotton gin, and built over eighty houses on the plantation including the Waters Mansion overlooking an orchard of pecan trees along the Brazos River. Arcola Plantation even had a shipping wharf on the Brazos River. By 1850, he had acquired the entire David Fitzgerald estate, while the Karankawa tribe had retreated to Mexico.

Sugar House

Waters later became a major stockholder and president of the Buffalo Bayou, Brazos, and Colorado Railway, which was incorporated in 1850 and began operations in 1855. The Houston Tap and Brazoria Railroad, incorporated on September 1, 1856, was constructed through the plantation area in 1858. The Gulf, Colorado & Santa Fe, International & Great Northern, and Sugarland Railroads also passed through the plantation. The plantation's cane trains, consisting of one sixteen-ton locomotive, fifty-five five-ton, and eighteen ten-ton cars, traversed over three miles of private railroad tracks. A spur from the main track of the International & Great Northern Railroads ran directly to the Sugar House, providing two shipping points. The House and Duke stations were located on the Arcola Plantation.

According to the 1860 Census, Johnathon Dawson Waters was the third-largest slaveholder in Texas, owning 216 enslaved people. By this time, Waters had become one of the wealthiest individuals in Fort Bend County. In 1863, he purchased the Waters-Moody Colonial Galveston Mansion, which served as a Confederate hospital during the Civil War. Additionally, Waters donated $100,000 in gold to the Confederacy, provided supplies and shelter for Confederate troops, and invested in bonds to finance the war effort.

However, the Confederacy's defeat in the Civil War resulted in significant financial losses for Waters, as the plantation economy, which was closely tied to slavery, had been a substantial driver of his wealth. After the war, Waters faced severe financial difficulties. His substantial support for the Confederacy, including the large donation in gold, significantly depleted his resources. The aftermath of the war and the ensuing economic turmoil further strained his finances, leading to his eventual bankruptcy despite his prior prosperity.

Slavery was an economic institution that relied on free labor to produce cash crops for profit. The average price of an enslaved person, regardless of age, sex, or condition, rose from approximately $400 in 1850 to nearly $800 by 1860. During the late 1850s, prime male field hands ages eighteen to thirty cost, on average, $1,200, and skilled enslaved people, such as blacksmiths, were often valued at over $2,000. In comparison, good quality Texas cotton land could be purchased for as little as six dollars per acre.

June 19, 1865, marks one of history's most significant social revolutions. The value of property owned by Southerners dropped by nearly 75%. This decline was particularly severe for personal property, with the wealthiest 10% of Southerners experiencing a 90% decrease in the value of their possessions. In contrast, the value of real estate decreased by approximately 50%.

Plantations in Texas faced significant challenges after the Civil War due to the loss of slave labor and a dramatic decline in land prices. Many wealthy plantation owners were in serious financial trouble, having invested heavily in the war effort. The availability of labor for the fields was nearly nonexistent, as many formerly enslaved individuals left the plantations in search family and better opportunities. Some relocated to cities or towns, while others moved to rural areas to start farms, businesses, or trades. Although a few chose to remain on the plantations, many became sharecroppers, renting land to farm independently.

Burnside Switch

Texas Convict Labor System

The Thirteenth Amendment to the United States Constitution clarified that the Emancipation Proclamation did not apply to formerly enslaved individuals who had been convicted of crimes and subsequently imprisoned. As a result, the state government of Texas developed a system to incarcerate Freedmen to regain access to a low-cost labor force reminiscent of slave labor, ultimately aiming to boost the state's economy. The amendment granted Texas the legal authority to exploit Freedmen through the Convict Leasing System beginning in 1866. This constitutional loophole paved the way for Texas lawmakers to establish a system of carceral labor.

In 1866, the Texas Legislature began debating how to reduce costs and overcrowding in the state prison system. These early discussions laid the groundwork for the convict leasing system. *On November 9, 1866, the Texas Legislature passed laws authorizing counties to employ incarcerated individuals in public works or lease them to private employers.*

By 1867, the first formal leases were executed when the Houston & Texas Central Railway and the Texas & Pacific Railway contracted with the state to use prison labor for infrastructure projects. What began with railroads quickly expanded into agriculture, with sugar planters becoming dominant beneficiaries. By the late 1860s, the Imperial Sugar Factory, later Imperial Sugar Company, had secured control over most nonviolent prisoners from the Texas Prison System and began subleasing them to other sugar and cotton plantations, including Arcola Plantation. These plantations operated under the Texas Convict Labor System, which granted the state complete control over the convicts, including their feeding, clothing, and supervision at the state's expense.

At Arcola Plantation, living quarters were provided for both guards and convicts, accommodating up to 175 convicts. A small plot of land was set aside for gardening to help sustain them. Waters leased convicts from the state for $31 per convict per month, and a sergeant lived in nearby quarters to supervise them. To help organize and streamline fieldwork, a convict camp known as Burnside Camp was established about 1.5 miles from the main quarters. According to Bill Griffen's 1936 biography, *the workforce at Arcola Plantation slightly increased during harvest season; out of 450 available workers, only about 140 were convicts.*

Prison Trustee Merrick

The plantation also provided housing for resident laborers: around fifty cabins for Black workers, a boarding house, and quarters for Mexican laborers. A comfortable residence was reserved for the general overseer. In Texas, plantation owners and businessmen profited significantly from the convict leasing system, while the State funneled profits into the treasury.

Before emancipation, the enslaved population grew much faster than that of whites because many plantation owners gained their wealth through dependence on slave labor. However, by 1876, 62 percent of the workers were white and 38 percent Black. Freedmen were employed on farms, as sharecroppers, owned land, or were imprisoned.

Following Waters's death on July 3, 1871, his wife, Martha Byne McGowen, sold the Arcola Plantation to Thomas Pierce for $50,000. A week later, Pierce sold the plantation to Houston businessman Thomas William House for $100,000. House had relocated to Houston, Texas, in 1838 and eventually became one of the wealthiest individuals in the state. He founded several companies, including House and Loveridge, Bakers and Confectioners, and owned property in as many as sixty-three counties across Texas. His most notable asset was the Arcola Sugar Plantation in Fort Bend County.

John Rutherford Fenn managed the plantation, and under his leadership, it expanded from the Brazos River to Oyster Creek, encompassing thousands of acres. In 1876, Fenn purchased seventy-five acres of land from Jane Perry. In 1885, he purchased one-third of the Thomas Barnett League from the Shipman Estate.

House's business ventures were extensive, including general merchandise, cotton brokerage, and banking. He was instrumental in organizing the Houston and Galveston Navigation Company and promoting the city's first street railway. Additionally, he organized the Board of Trade and Cotton Exchange and the Houston Gas Light Company. House's influence was also felt in the railroad industry, where he served as a director and stockholder in several companies.

Thomas William House was elected as the 4th Ward alderman for
Houston in 1857 and again in 1861. In 1862, he became the mayor of
Houston. He passed away on January 17, 1880. After his death,
House's estate continued to operate various businesses, including the
T. W. House Bank and the Arcola Sugar Mills Company.

Arcola Sugar Mills Company Incorporation

The Arcola Sugar Mills Company, Inc. was originally incorporated under Texas law in 1899, with Thomas William House, Jr. as its principal organizer and the former Arcola Plantation as its nucleus. On March 18, 1903, the company underwent a formal reorganization or recapitalization, issuing 7,500 shares of stock at $100 each, totaling $750,000 in capital. This 1903 filing, often misinterpreted as the date of original incorporation, reflects a significant corporate milestone but not the founding of the entity itself.

The company's stated purpose was to cultivate sugarcane, manufacture sugar, and establish a dominant position in the Gulf Coast sugar market. As part of its formation, the company acquired the existing mill, machinery, and thousands of acres of fertile land along Oyster Creek. The mill was designed to process cane grown in company-owned fields and on neighboring farmers' land, positioning Arcola as a regional hub for industrial sugar production.

Court filings and estate records confirm his role as incorporator and initial shareholder, contributing land, capital, and management expertise from Arcola Plantation as the nucleus of the new company. Contemporary reports strongly suggest that other incorporators included members of the House family and close business associates tied to Houston's banking and mercantile networks. What is clear from the official record is that the House family held the first major block of shares, positioning Thomas W. House, Jr. as the statutory patriarch of the enterprise and anchoring Arcola's bid to rival Louisiana in sugar production. Optimism was high: many believed Texas could rival Louisiana in sugar output, and Arcola Plantation's strategic location and infrastructure made it a centerpiece of that vision.

Under House, Arcola Plantation expanded its sugar operations and became one of the state's principal convict-leased plantations.

Contractors like Ward, Dewey & Co. held full control of the penitentiary system in the early 1870s, granting lessees total authority over prisoners' labor, housing, and discipline. Conditions were brutal, mortality was high, and convicts were housed in segregated barracks near the fields.

Arcola Plantation's Burnside quarters, established during the height of convict leasing, were located approximately 1.5 miles from the main plantation residence and mill complex. This spatial separation reflected the rigid segregation of labor and oversight: convict laborers were housed in barracks near the fields, while guards and overseers lived closer to the main house. The quarters included a small garden plot for subsistence and were supervised by a sergeant stationed nearby.

During harvest season, the workforce expanded slightly, but the convict population remained the backbone of Arcola's sugar operations.

Adjacent to these quarters, Burnside Cemetery emerged as a burial site for both enslaved individuals and incarcerated laborers. Graves were unmarked, and no formal registry was maintained.

Local historians and community members have worked to document the site, noting its proximity to the convict camp and its absence from official records. The cemetery's continued invisibility in civic documentation reflects the broader erasure of carceral labor and Black burial grounds in Fort Bend County.

Thomas Howe Scanlan

Thomas Howe Scanlan was one of the largest depositors in the T.W. House Bank, and he was involved in House's business ventures, including the T.W. House Bank and the Arcola Sugar Mills Company. The Union government appointed Scanlan alderman of the third ward in 1868 and mayor of Houston in 1870 (City of Houston). During his time as mayor of Houston, Thomas Howe Scanlan made significant contributions to support Freedmen. He appointed four Freedmen out of ten aldermen on the city council, including Jason Rice and Taylor Burke, who represented Houston's First Ward. With these appointments, Scanlan actively promoted the election of Freedmen councilmen in 1872, which led to increased representation in local government. Richard Brock, appointed by Governor E.J. Davis in 1870, also served as an alderman.

In 1873, the Houston Police Department included six Colored and six white officers. Scanlan's efforts extended to ensure that Freedmen had opportunities to participate in public office and fulfill other civic duties. These actions were part of a broader movement aimed at integrating Black Americans into the political, economic, and social fabric of the South (Benham, Priscilla, 1995).

This broader push for inclusion and empowerment also found roots in Fort Bend County, where key Black leaders emerged to shape the era during Reconstruction and beyond. Walter Moses Burton, notably the first Black man elected as sheriff in the U.S. in 1869, later served as a Texas State Senator from 1874 to 1882. He was a strong advocate for public education and the establishment of schools for Black children.

Among his significant contributions was his role in pushing through legislation that led to the creation of Alta Vista Agricultural and Mechanical College of Texas for Colored Youth (Prairie View A&M University), established in 1876. Despite facing significant opposition from white political factions, particularly during the Jaybird-Woodpecker War, Burton became one of the richest men in Fort Bend County through land ownership and political influence.

Charles Ferguson graduated from Fisk University in Nashville, Tennessee, in 1880. He then moved to Fort Bend County with his brother, Henry Clay Ferguson, and began a career in government service. Ferguson lived in Richmond and owned a 1,500-acre plantation on Jones Creek. He was elected as the clerk of the district court in Fort Bend County in 1882, 1884, and 1886, although he did not complete the final year of his last term.

On September 6, 1888, Ferguson faced expulsion by the Jaybirds, a group that included members with white supremacist ideologies. He was given only ten hours to leave the county, a stark example of the extreme measures taken to suppress Black political power during that period. Despite this injustice, Ferguson made significant contributions to advancing Black representation and political influence during Reconstruction. Alongside James D. Davis, another Black leader who faced exile, Ferguson filed a civil rights lawsuit against the Jaybirds in federal court in Galveston in 1889. The case was settled out of court, with Ferguson receiving $13,000 in damages for the harm he endured.

Thomas Lane Taylor was the first Black County commissioner for Precinct 2 in Fort Bend County, serving from 1878 to 1882. During the Reconstruction era, he worked tirelessly to improve infrastructure, enhance public services, and advocate for the rights of Blacks. Taylor established roots as an agriculturist and cattle raiser, prospering and purchasing a homestead in Boone's Bend in Wharton County. Despite facing significant opposition, including threats and violence from groups like the Jaybirds, Taylor's legacy endures as a testament to his contributions to the community. His impact is commemorated through various tributes, including the naming of Thomas Taylor Parkway in Missouri City.

These leaders' resilience and dedication to improving the lives of Black people in Fort Bend County are noteworthy despite the significant challenges they faced. Their accomplishments and perseverance are a testament to their commitment to justice and equality.

Benjamin Franklin Williams was a pioneering Black legislator, minister, and civic leader whose life bridged slavery, emancipation, and Reconstruction-era governance in Texas. Born enslaved in Virginia, Williams was relocated through South Carolina and Tennessee before being brought to Texas in 1859. After emancipation, he joined the Methodist Episcopal Church and became a traveling minister, known for his powerful sermons and organizational leadership.

In 1865, Williams helped found Wesley Chapel Methodist Church in Austin, one of the earliest Freedmen's congregations in the state. His religious work quickly expanded into political advocacy. He was elected as a delegate to the 1868–69 Texas Constitutional Convention, where he served on the Executive Committee and proposed measures to ban racial segregation in public accommodations.

Williams went on to serve three terms in the Texas House of Representatives between 1870 and 1886, representing Fort Bend, Colorado, Lavaca, Waller, and Wharton counties. His legislative record included labor protections for agricultural workers and efforts to secure civil rights for Freedmen. He was a staunch Republican and a vice president of the Loyal Union League, a political organization that mobilized Black voters and kept white Unionists informed of Black civic activity.

Williams died in office in 1886 and was buried at Newman Chapel Cemetery near Kendleton, Texas, a Freedmen's town founded by formerly enslaved families who purchased land from the Kendall plantation. Benjamin Franklin Williams remains a foundational figure in Texas history, embodying the transition from bondage to political agency and leaving behind a legacy of faith, governance, and community-building.

John Rutherford Fenn

The House and Fenn families remained central to Arcola Plantation's operations, their lives intertwined with the plantation's labor and land. The death of John Rutherford Fenn in 1904 illustrates both the prominence of these families and the rituals that bound community memory to place. On November 24, 1904, John Rutherford Fenn, son of Sarah Fitzgerald and Eli Fenn, died in Houston. His funeral was held the following morning at 9:00 a.m. at the family residence, 1117 Bell Avenue. After the service, his body was transported to the International and Great Northern Depot, where a special train had been arranged by T. W. House, Jr., in cooperation with Leroy Trice of the International and Great Northern Railway. The train was designated to carry the funeral party to and from Duke, the station nearest Fenn's ranch and plantation. The Sugar Land Railway Company permitted the train to travel over its tracks from Arcola Junction to Duke.

Duke Road

Upon arrival, friends and neighbors gathered to pay their respects. They brought enough vehicles to accommodate the funeral party. A family carriage and driver had been sent from Houston for the widow's use on this final, sorrowful journey to the family burial ground, Duke Cemetery.

The cemetery had been established by William Paschal Hamblin on September 14, 1901, following the death of his mother, Jane Hogue Hamblin. It was located in the southern half of the western two-thirds of the old Perry homestead. W. P. Hamblin was the son of Jane Hogue Hamblin and Daniel Perry.

A brief stop was made at Fenn's house in Duke to allow family, servants, and plantation workers, some of whom had served the family for five generations, to pay their respects and bid farewell to their old marse.

At the burial site, Dr. William Hayne Leavell of the First Presbyterian Church conducted a brief service of readings and prayers. John Rutherford Fenn was laid to rest beneath the tall live oaks of Duke Cemetery, their branches draped in gray moss. After the final rites, the funeral party returned to Houston on the special train, arriving around 3:45 p.m. (*Houston Post*, November 25, 1904).

Within two years, another passing would reshape Houston's civic and financial landscape. In 1906, Thomas Howe Scanlan died, and his seven unmarried daughters inherited his substantial estate. Their claims positioned the Scanlan heirs to receive a significant portion of the reorganized assets.

The national banking panic of 1907, triggered by the Knickerbocker Trust collapse in New York, destabilized Houston's financial houses. The estate of Thomas William House collapsed under debts approaching $2 million, drawing in nearly two thousand creditors. A smaller group, initially representing about $300,000 in claims, met in the office of Judge Edwin Paschal Hamblen to prepare for the sale of the bankrupt estate's properties. They resolved to act collectively by

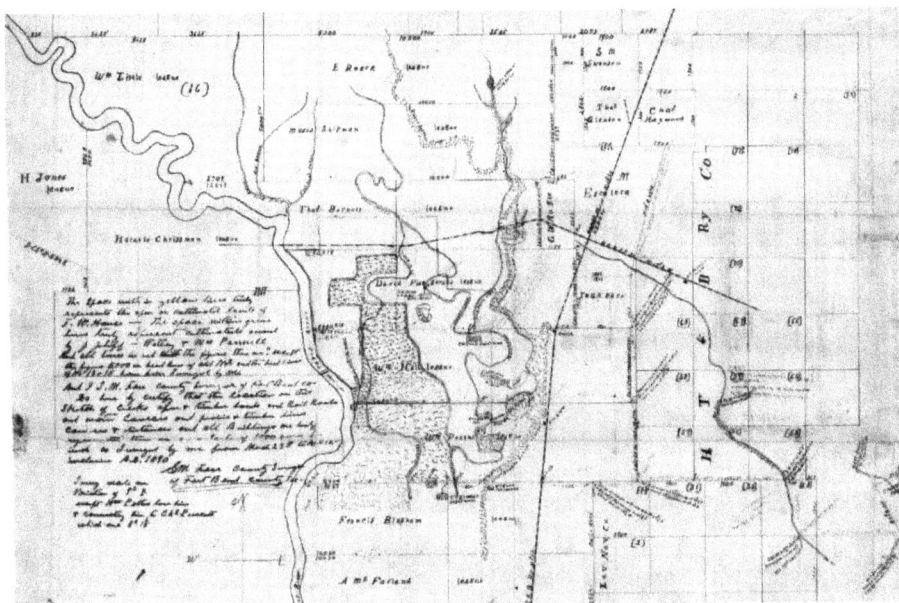

Arcola Sugar Plantation on Oyster Creek Map

forming a stock company and named Miss Kate Scanlan, Henry Albrecht, and Andrew Dow as trustees, authorizing them to submit bids at the public auction scheduled for ten o'clock at the House residence on Franklin Avenue and Fannin Street.

The sale was conducted under the supervision of Trustee J. S. Rice, who reported the results to Referee in Bankruptcy J. J. Borden. Three parties appeared as bidders: the creditors' trustees representing the stock company, independent bidder F. E. Arnim, and Kobe & McKinnon of Chicago, acting for the Chicago Asset Realization Company. After competitive bidding, the creditors' cooperative succeeded in acquiring the estate's holdings, including Houston city properties, the Arcola Plantation, and tracts across Texas, for $860,000.

By 1908, investigative journalists and reformers exposed the brutality of convict leasing in Texas. Reports documented starvation, beatings, and mortality rates that rivaled slavery. The Houston Chronicle and

Dallas Morning News carried accounts of *men worked to death in the cane fields and children incarcerated alongside hardened criminals.* Legislative committees in 1908–1909 held hearings where witnesses described corruption in contracts and deaths unreported to the state.

Governor Thomas M. Campbell, elected in 1906, was a reform Democrat aligned with James Hogg's populist tradition. He distrusted monopolistic business interests and emphasized labor protections. In his 1909 address to the Texas Legislature, Campbell declared: *The leasing of human beings for profit is a disgrace to Texas. The penitentiary should not be a marketplace for flesh, but an institution for reform and humane discipline.*

Legislative debates in 1909 centered on whether to abolish leasing outright or reform it. Planters and industrialists argued that abolition would bankrupt the prison system and devastate agricultural output.

Reformers countered with testimony from physicians, clergy, and former guards who described *systemic abuse, corruption in contracts, and deaths unreported to the state.* The House Committee on

Penitentiaries issued a report detailing overcrowded barracks, lack of medical care, and disciplinary practices that included whipping, shackling, and starvation.

PRISON POPULATION BY RACE
1880-1912

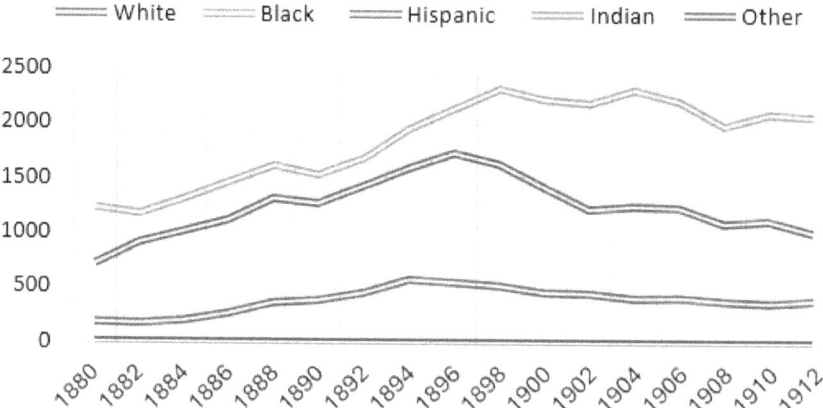

The Texas Penitentiary System housed approximately 4,000 inmates, though facilities like Huntsville and Rusk could only accommodate about half that number. Over 75 percent of convicts were leased to private enterprises, including sugar plantations, cotton farms, railroad construction sites, and mining operations. This leasing system generated substantial revenue: lessees paid the state over $358,000 during the leasing era, while retaining more than $500,000 in profits. Agricultural labor dominated the system; by 1884, for example, 1,148 prisoners were contracted to farms, compared to just 176 on railroads, and this pattern continued into the early 1900s. These figures confirm that convict leasing remained the backbone of Texas's prison labor economy until Governor Campbell's reforms in 1910.

Campbell's administration responded with legislation in 1910 that abolished private leasing and created the State Account System. Under this model, convicts worked on state-owned farms such as Wynne, Harlem, and Imperial, producing cotton, corn, and sugar under direct state supervision. The goal was to eliminate profit-driven abuse while maintaining agricultural output. Though carceral agriculture continued, private leasing was formally ended.

The Penitentiary Commission attempted to revive agricultural output by leasing 3,600 acres of Arcola Plantation land at $7 per acre, claiming half of mill profits and holding a $550,000 purchase option. Convicts were supplied directly by the prison system, with T. W. House, Jr. retained as manager. The experiment failed almost immediately: droughts and freezes devastated crops, the mill was outdated, and productivity was low. The State never exercised its option.

In 1909, the Scanlan sisters completed the Scanlan Building in downtown Houston, one of the city's first fireproof skyscrapers. Located at Main and Preston, the building was financed in part by profits redirected from Arcola Sugar Mills Company and other plantation holdings. Estate records show that dividends from sugar operations and land leases were invested into urban real estate and Catholic infrastructure. The building housed law offices, civic organizations, and Catholic charities, reflecting the sisters' dual commitment to commercial development and religious mission. Its construction marked a deliberate shift in the family's investment strategy, from agricultural extraction to urban permanence, and symbolized the transfer of wealth from rural labor to metropolitan influence.

By 1911, the Scanlan Estate had acquired controlling interest in Arcola Sugar Mills Company, Inc., purchasing 7,100 of the 7,500 shares for $450,000. Kate Scanlan assumed the dual role of president and treasurer, while her sisters Lillian and Stella served as directors, giving Kate Scanlan and her sisters overwhelming corporate control.

Corporate control was not enough. The creditors' trustees sold Arcola

Plantation, 8,000 acres, including a farm at Arcola station on the Columbia Tap division of the International and Great Northern Railway, to Kate Scanlan and her sisters for $500,000. The court confirmed the sale. Their purchase ended the State's leasehold and extinguished the purchase option.

Unlike the State, the Scanlans did not attempt to revive sugar cultivation at scale. The Scanlans quickly abandoned sugar cultivation.

By 1914, cane fields were gone, and in 1915, storm-damaged machinery was sold off. Arcola's prominence faded after the end of sugar cultivation and the State lease. Once a principal town in Fort Bend County, Arcola was eclipsed by Sugar Land's rise as the center of carceral agriculture and industrial sugar production.

According to Fort Bend County records and local histories, the Arcola school district maintained segregated schools for Black children well into the 20th century. These schools were located on and near the Arcola Plantation itself, serving families who had remained in the community after emancipation. The 1917 Fort Bend County school census documented Black children enrolled in these schools even after sugar cultivation ended in 1914, with the termination of the state convict lease system. Their placement near the plantation's residential quarters reflected the continuity of settlement and labor: the Scanlan family continued housing and employing Black workers through the 1930s, and the schools provided education for their children.

Between 1913 and 1917, sisters Lillian and Stella Scanlan, devout Catholics, constructed the Sacred Heart Chapel near their home at 714 Scanlan Road, Arcola. At their request, the Missionary Catechists of Divine Providence from San Antonio came to provide religious education for children in the area. The chapel quickly became a hub of Catholic life for the local population, many of whom worked on the plantation. By the 1920s, chapel activities were firmly established. Priests from Houston and Sugar Land visited regularly, First Communion became a major annual event, and the sisters provided food, clothing, and support for children and nuns alike.

On April 14, 1927, the Arcola Sugar Mills Company deeded a tract of land to Fort Bend County for use as a cemetery, now known as House Plantation Cemetery (29.49967° N, –95.51689° W, NAD83), located on McKeever Road in Sugar Land within the Thomas Barnett League. On the same date, the company sold an adjoining parcel to the Gulf, Colorado & Santa Fe Railroad Company for right-of-way through the same league. These transactions marked the estate's shift away from sugar and toward civic and infrastructural uses, preserving burial grounds tied to plantation families while enabling regional railroad expansion.

On October 10, 1933, stockholder D.H. Burnham sued the Arcola Sugar Mills Company, alleging abandonment of operations and mismanagement by Kate Scanlan, the principal stockholder. The lower court initially ordered dissolution and appointed Burnham receiver. On December 15, 1933, however, the U.S. Court of Appeals for the Fifth Circuit reversed the dissolution order, ruling that Burnham could receive compensation for his shares without terminating the corporation.

Kate Scanlan died on April 26, 1936. After her death, the Scanlan sisters assumed management of the estate. In 1937, Stella wrote: *We must ensure the children have a place to learn and pray. The chapel will be their sanctuary.* Estate ledgers from this year record disbursements for food, medical care, and stipends for visiting priests, underscoring their vision of the plantation as a site of Catholic mission and community care.

In 1938, the Arcola Plantation was formally reorganized into cattle ranching, with pastures replacing cane fields and woodlands reclaiming former farmland. That same year, an oil lease was recorded on a tract near the Brazos River under a ten-year agreement with a Houston drilling company. The decline of sugar reduced the need for large seasonal workforces, prompting many Black laborers to move into ranch work or leave the area altogether. Housing once reserved for cane workers was vacated or repurposed, and the estate ceased building new cabins. Oral testimony and archival records suggest that some families relocated to nearby towns for industrial or domestic employment, while others remained on marginal plots with limited infrastructure. This gradual outmigration marked the end of Arcola's era as a labor-intensive plantation and mirrored broader changes in rural Black settlement across Fort Bend County.

In 1946, the Cenacle Sisters formally affiliated with the Congregation of Divine Providence, continuing their work on the plantation.

Foundation, Sale, and Erasure

On January 25, 1947, Scanlan's youngest daughters, Lillian and Stella, entrusted the estate to the Scanlan Foundation. The foundation charter, filed with the State of Texas, listed Lillian and Stella Scanlan as founding trustees and defined its mission as *the advancement of Catholic education, worship, and charitable works throughout the Diocese of Galveston-Houston.* The foundation then began managing the property and concentrated on charitable activities, primarily supporting Catholic institutions and initiatives.

Archival photographs from 1950 depict the Sacred Heart Chapel as the community's primary worship site, though it remained a mission station under St. Theresa's in Sugar Land and later Manvel.

On June 29, 1969, the parish was formally consecrated at the present church in Manvel, officiated by Bishop John Morkovsky.

In 1971, the Scanlan Foundation sold 8,000 acres of the Scanlan Ranch (Arcola Plantation) for about $9.6 million to Fuqua Industries,

Inc. of Atlanta, Georgia. Internal correspondence from the Foundation cited declining agricultural returns and rising maintenance costs as the rationale for the sale. Proceeds were earmarked for the expansion of Catholic schools and diocesan facilities in Houston.

The Catholic Diocese of Houston used the plantation and the Scanlan mansion at 714 Scanlan Road as a Cenacle Retreat until 1972. The Cenacle Sisters named the retreat *Siena* in honor of St. Catherine of Siena, the patron saint of single women and spiritual contemplation. The name also referenced the Siena region of Italy, known for its clay-rich soil, which produces the pigment *sienna* used in oil and watercolor painting. This naming choice reflected both the spiritual mission of the retreat and the earthy tones of the surrounding landscape. Importantly, the name *Siena* applied only to the immediate house site and its use as a Catholic retreat, not to the broader Arcola Plantation lands. The full 8,000-acre tract remained legally and historically known as Arcola Plantation until its sale in 1971.

In 1978, the property was acquired by Johnson Development

Corporation. The new owners, Johnson Corporation, AFC Pacific Properties, and Thompson Lake Partners, began development plans, renaming the entire project Siena Plantation.

By the 1990s, preservationists and community members raised concerns about the fate of Arcola's historic lands, cemeteries, and water infrastructure. While the Scanlan House was retained as a symbolic centerpiece, no formal preservation easement was recorded, and much of the surrounding landscape was regraded for suburban development. In the months leading up to the 1996 groundbreaking, Fort Bend County historians and preservation advocates submitted letters to the developer and county commissioners requesting a formal preservation easement for the Scanlan House and surrounding acreage.

One letter, signed by members of the Fort Bend Historical Commission, stated: *The Arcola Plantation is one of the last remaining sites directly tied to Texas's convict leasing system. Its preservation is not optional; it is a moral obligation.*

Despite these efforts, development pressures prevailed. The developer responded that the house would be *retained as a symbolic centerpiece,* but offered no legal protections or interpretive signage. Community members expressed concern that the plantation's legacy, including its ties to carceral labor, Black education, and Catholic stewardship, would be erased in favor of suburban branding. The absence of formal protections reflected a broader pattern of historical erasure in Fort Bend County's development practices. On March 9, 1996, the developers held a groundbreaking ceremony at the Scanlan House. From that moment, Arcola's transformation from historic plantation to suburban subdivision was irreversible. Developers later demolished the Scanlan House in 2017.

Over the years, the land at Arcola Plantation on Oyster Creek was sold or repurposed for residential and commercial use. What was once the core of the Arcola Sugar Mills Company became integrated into the surrounding areas, including the 10,800-acre Sienna master-planned community, Burlington Northern Santa Fe Railway, Missouri City, Arcola, Hawdon, Juliff, and Duke.

The story of Arcola Plantation is not simply about one tract of land in Fort Bend County. It embodies the larger arc of Texas history: the exploitation of enslaved and incarcerated labor, the collapse of financial empires, the stewardship of Catholic women who redirected wealth into community care, and the eventual erasure of that legacy under suburban development. Each stage reveals how power, labor, and memory were contested, repurposed, and often obscured.

Preserving this record restores visibility to the Black families, convict laborers, and Catholic stewards whose lives shaped Arcola, ensuring that their contributions are not lost beneath the veneer of modern growth.

Carceral Cemeteries

Across Fort Bend County, the legacy of convict leasing is etched not only into the fields and mills but into the burial grounds that remain largely undocumented, unmarked, and unprotected.

Three cemeteries, Burnside, Imperial, and Sugar Land 95, stand as silent witnesses to the carceral labor system that shaped the region's agricultural economy and racial hierarchy. Each site reflects a distinct phase of institutional control, civic neglect, and descendant resilience.

Burnside Cemetery (Arcola Plantation)

Located approximately 1.5 miles from the main residence and mill complex at Arcola Plantation, Burnside Cemetery is believed to be the burial ground for both enslaved individuals and incarcerated laborers. Established during the height of convict leasing, the cemetery sits adjacent to the segregated barracks that housed leased convicts working the cane fields. Graves were unmarked, and no formal registry was maintained. The site does not appear on county cemetery maps and has never been formally surveyed or protected. Its location has been preserved primarily through oral testimony and descendant

44

memory, with local historians and community members working to document its existence. Burnside's invisibility in civic documentation reflects the broader erasure of Black burial grounds and carceral death in Fort Bend County.

Imperial Cemetery (Imperial State Prison Farm)

The Imperial Cemetery, formally known as the Old Imperial Farm Cemetery, was established in 1912 on the grounds of the Imperial State Prison Farm in Sugar Land. It served as the burial site for incarcerated laborers who died while working under the convict leasing system and later under state-run agricultural operations. Located near Highway 6 and US 90-A, the cemetery contains at least thirty-one confirmed graves, most of them Black men. Like Burnside, Imperial's cemetery remained largely unmarked and unacknowledged for decades. Though tied to one of Texas's earliest state-owned prison farms, the site was excluded from public memory and civic preservation efforts until recent advocacy prompted limited recognition. The cemetery's proximity to the Imperial Sugar complex underscores the entwinement of carceral labor and industrial sugar production in Fort Bend County.

Sugar Land 95 (Imperial Farm Prison No. 2)

In 2018, construction crews preparing a site for a new school in Sugar Land uncovered the remains of ninety-five Black prisoners buried in unmarked graves. The site, located on the grounds of the former Imperial Farm Prison No. 2, became known as the Sugar Land 95.

These individuals were victims of the convict leasing system, forced to labor under brutal conditions in the cane fields of Fort Bend County. Their discovery sparked public outcry and renewed scrutiny of Texas's carceral past. Unlike Burnside and Imperial, Sugar Land 95 received formal archaeological investigation and limited memorialization, though debates over interpretation, descendant consultation, and civic accountability continue. The graves were eventually reinterred, but the site remains a focal point for discussions about historical erasure, racial violence, and the legacy of forced labor in Texas.

Together, Burnside, Imperial, and Sugar Land 95 form a triad of carceral cemeteries, each shaped by institutional neglect and community memory. Their continued invisibility in official records and development plans reflects the unresolved tension between economic expansion and historical truth. These burial grounds demand not only recognition but reparative stewardship, grounded in descendant testimony and civic accountability.

Texas Land Grants and Settlement

Throughout history, various governing bodies, including Spain, Mexico, the Republic of Texas, and the State of Texas, issued land grants to promote settlement and development in the region. During the Republic of Texas, several types of land grants were awarded, including headright grants for settlers, military grants for soldiers, and preemption grants that allowed settlers to purchase land at a reduced price.

Spanish and Mexican Periods (1600-1821)

In the 18th century, the Spanish Crown and the Mexican government issued land grants to encourage settlement and cattle ranching. In 1519, Spanish explorer Alonso Álvarez de Pineda mapped the Texas coastline. In 1685, French explorer Robert Cavelier, Sieur de La Salle, mistakenly landed in Texas and established Fort St. Louis. This prompted Spain to set up missions and settlements in East Texas to counter French influence. Notably, in 1718, Spanish missionaries founded San Antonio, and in 1731, the San Antonio de Valero Mission (later known as The Alamo) was established. Spain governed Texas as part of the Viceroyalty of New Spain.

In 1821, Mexico gained independence from Spain, and Texas became part of Mexico. Stephen F. Austin and other empresarios received grants from the Mexican government, bringing settlers to Texas and fostering the region's development.

Indian Tribes

Before European colonization, Texas was home to numerous Indian tribes, such as the Caddo, Karankawa, Apache, and Comanche. These tribes had diverse cultures and ways of life, ranging from agricultural societies to nomadic hunters and gatherers.

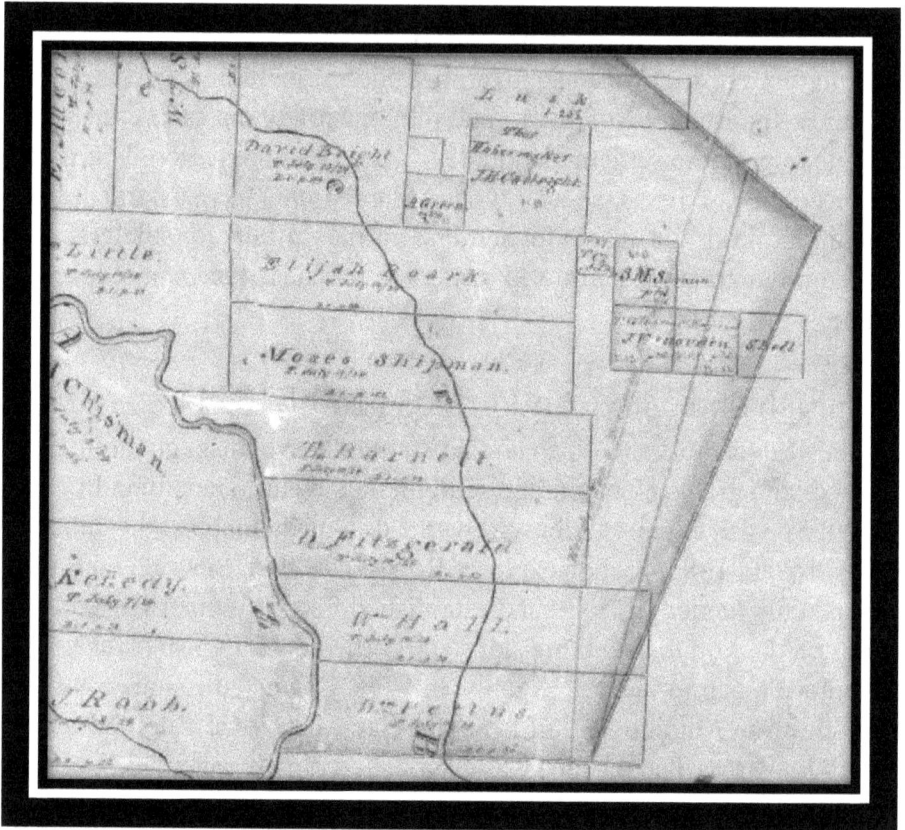

Upshur, Horace L. Fort Bend County, map, 1839

Republic of Texas (1836-1845)

The 1836 Constitution specified that all heads of families living in Texas on March 4, 1836, except for Africans and Indians, were eligible for land grants. However, notable exceptions were made for military service. Military land grants in Texas served as compensation and incentives for soldiers. Depending on their service, soldiers could receive headright grants or preemption grants. Bounty and Donation Warrants allowed soldiers to claim up to 1,280 acres through Bounty Warrants or 640 acres through Donation Warrants. These grants could be sold or developed by the soldiers. If soldiers did not claim their Bounty and Donation Warrants within the designated timeframe, the land became available for others. The Texas Court of Claims was established to manage such cases and assess claims against the Republic and the state. Unclaimed land could be forfeited and granted to other eligible individuals.

No free person of African descent, either in whole or in part, shall be permitted to reside in the Republic of Texas without the consent of Congress.

1836 Constitution of the Republic of Texas

The 1836 Constitution also granted *first-class* headrights of one league and one labor (4,605.5 acres) to heads of families and one-third of a league (1,476.1 acres) to single men. Despite the general exclusion, a few notable Black individuals claimed land during the Republic of Texas. William Goyens, a free Black man who migrated from North Carolina to Texas in the early 1820s, became a prominent blacksmith near Nacogdoches and played a significant role as an interpreter for Sam Houston with the East Texas Indians. Samuel McCulloch, Jr., believed to have been the first casualty of the Texas Revolution, also claimed land. These individuals and others contributed to the early history of Texas despite the challenges they faced.

The Republic of Texas also issued a few colonization contracts, the last of which was the Mercer colony, created by a contract signed on January 29, 1844. Upon Texas's annexation to the United States, the Convention of 1845 called for the end of colony contracts.

State of Texas (1845-Present)

Following annexation, Texas used land grants to incentivize railroad construction. The 1876 Texas Constitution authorized railroads 8 sections of public land for every mile of track they laid, which was later increased to 16 sections per mile in 1854 and 20 sections per mile after the Civil War.

During the period when the U.S. Homestead Act of 1862 was in effect, Blacks and Indians faced significant barriers to accessing its benefits. Discriminatory practices and legal obstacles often prevented them from successfully claiming land. However, some Black Americans, referred to as Freedmen during this period, benefited, with approximately 3,500 homesteaders successfully claiming land and obtaining patents (titles) for around 650,000 acres.

In Fort Bend County, Texas, Black homesteaders established several Freedom Colonies, forming self-sufficient agrarian communities. These settlements were created by formerly enslaved individuals and their descendants seeking economic independence and safety from racial terror. These Freedom Colonies played a crucial role in preserving Freedmen's cultural heritage in the region. Today, the legacy of these communities continues to influence property rights and land use in Fort Bend.

However, the situation was more complex for Indians. While the Homestead Act did not explicitly exclude them, its implementation often led to their displacement and loss of traditional lands. Many Indian tribes were forced onto reservations, and the act contributed to the further fragmentation of their land holdings. However, some Indians did attempt to adapt to the new land laws and sought opportunities within the framework of the Homestead Act.

By 1882, the legislature repealed the land grant law as unappropriated land dwindled. These grants had been crucial for developing Texas' railroad infrastructure, though they were sometimes marred by political manipulation and fraud. The discovery of oil at Spindletop in

1901 sparked a new wave of land acquisitions, transforming Texas's economy. During the subsequent oil boom, land acquisition focused on leasing mineral rights. Oil companies identified promising areas, negotiated leases with landowners, and offered royalty percentages for drilling rights. Mineral rights were often separate from surface rights, leading to formal agreements outlining lease terms.

However, this era also saw instances of fraud, such as Ponzi schemes and misrepresentation of project potential. In Fort Bend County, Texas, Black communities faced significant environmental injustices, experiencing pollution, health hazards, and economic exploitation due to the proximity of oil refineries and chemical plants. These refineries were often located near predominantly Black neighborhoods, leading to higher exposure to toxic emissions and related health issues.

CROSSING
ROAD

The International-Great Northern Railroad
The International Railroad Company

The International Railroad Company was chartered on August 5, 1870, with an ambitious vision to construct a railway from the south bank of the Red River, near Fulton, Arkansas, to Laredo, Texas, with plans for expansion into Mexico. This bold initiative was overseen by a board of directors, including notable figures such as Thomas William House, John S. Kennedy, Henry G. Marquand, H.W. Grey, Thomas W. Pearsall, Paul N. Spofford, James W. Barnes, William Walter Phelps, and John S. Barnes. On October 9, 1870, the company's board elected John S. Kennedy as President, Thomas William House as Financial Agent, Thomas W. Pearsall as Treasurer, Paul N. Spofford as

Secretary, and James W. Barnes as Vice President. They organized the company with a capital stock of $2 million, with 20 percent paid in the first assessment.

However, the International Railroad Company was involved in instances of fraud. In 1871, the Texas Supreme Court ruled that the company had engaged in fraudulent activities related to the issuance of bonds. The court found that the company had not met the requirements outlined in its charter and associated amendments, and as a result, the bonds issued were deemed unconstitutional. Specifically, the ruling stated that the company failed to construct the railway as required by its charter, which included a timeline for progress on the construction. As a result, the court concluded that the company forfeited its rights to the lands granted under the act, thus relieving the state of Texas from any future obligations to provide land or grant tax exemptions to the company.

This ruling highlighted the fraudulent practices in enacting the law that allowed the issuance of these bonds. The fraudulent activities included stock watering, the practice of inflating the value of a company's stock to attract investors, often by misrepresenting the company's financial health or potential, and land speculation, involving the purchase of large tracts of land with the expectation that its value would increase, often through manipulation or insider information, and then selling it at a profit. Nevertheless, the company remained determined and by 1873, had successfully built 177 miles of track.

The Houston and Great Northern Railroad

The Houston and Great Northern Railroad chartered on October 22, 1866, encountered several significant challenges during its construction and early years. Despite financial difficulties stemming from the financial panic of 1873, political and social instability during the Reconstruction period, and numerous logistical hurdles, including sourcing materials and labor shortages, the company established a line from Houston to the Red River and beyond. Building the railroad across Texas's diverse and often rugged terrain required overcoming natural obstacles like rivers and swamps.

The Houston and Great Northern Railroad also faced allegations of stock watering and land speculation. These practices misled investors and the public, leading to significant financial abuse and contributing to the railroad's financial difficulties.

Furthermore, the Texas Supreme Court ruling against issuing $2 million in bonds for the International Railroad Company due to constitutional issues concerning state land grants also affected the Houston and Great Northern Railroad, complicating their financial situation further.

Nevertheless, the railroad persevered and successfully completed 253 miles of track by 1873, playing a crucial role in the development of Texas's transportation infrastructure. Early organizers, including notable figures such as Ebenezar B. Nichols, William Marsh Rice, W. J. Hutchins, H. D. Taylor, and B. A. Shepherd, oversaw the project's progression.

On September 30, 1873, the Houston and Great Northern Railroad consolidated with the International Railroad Company to form the International-Great Northern Railroad, which continued to expand and eventually became part of the Missouri Pacific lines.

The International-Great Northern Railroad

The International-Great Northern Railroad Company was formed on September 30, 1873, through the merger of the International Railroad Company and the Houston and Great Northern Railroad. This consolidation created a significant rail network in Texas, with the International Railroad Company initially operating 177 miles of track from Hearne to Longview and the Houston and Great Northern Railroad contributing 252 miles of track (Missouri Pacific Historical Society).

PALESTINE, TEXAS
1892

The initial board members of the International Railroad Company included John S. Barnes (President), James W. Barnes, Paul N. Spofford, and Thomas W. House. From the Houston and Great Northern Railroad, board members such as Charles G. Young (President), E. C. Stockton (Secretary), and P. J. Willis (Treasurer) were also elected to the board. Both John S. Barnes and Charles G. Young served as presidents, combining their leadership to guide the newly formed International-Great Northern Railroad Company through its early years and expansion.

Their combined expertise and leadership facilitated the expansion of the International-Great Northern Railroad Company, connecting Rockdale in 1874, Austin in 1876, and eventually San Antonio and Laredo by 1881. Despite the financial panic of 1873, the company continued to grow and became a vital part of Texas's transportation infrastructure.

The Panic of 1873 was a severe financial crisis that triggered an economic depression in Europe and North America, lasting from 1873 to 1877 or 1879 in some regions. The crisis had multiple underlying causes, including rampant speculative investments (especially in railroads), American inflation, the demonetization of silver in Germany and the United States, economic dislocation in Europe due to the Franco-Prussian War, and significant property losses in the Great Chicago Fire (1871) and the Great Boston Fire (1872).

The first symptoms of the crisis appeared in Vienna, Austria-Hungary, where financial failures spread to most of Europe and North America by 1873. In the United States, the panic led to widespread bank failures, with at least one hundred banks failing. A significant trigger was the stock market crash in Vienna on May 9, 1873. In the United States, the crisis was exacerbated by overinvestment in railroads.

The collapse of Jay Cooke & Company, a major financier of railroad construction, on September 18, 1873, led to a nationwide panic. The panic resulted in a prolonged economic depression, with many businesses failing and high unemployment rates. By 1876, unemployment had risen to 14 percent. Despite the financial panic of 1873, the International-Great Northern Railroad Company continued to grow and became a vital part of Texas's transportation infrastructure.

However, the railroad faced several challenges, including financial difficulties leading to receivership in 1908 due to the Panic of 1907, which caused a significant economic downturn impacting many businesses. The first receivership involved a trustee managing the company's assets and operations to pay off its debts. Despite efforts to stabilize the company.

The International-Great Northern Railroad Company faced ongoing financial difficulties and could not meet its debt obligations. The company entered receivership again in 1922. This process highlighted the company's ongoing financial instability. Due to the inability to recover financially, the company was sold at foreclosure on July 31, 1922—the foreclosure sale aimed to settle the company's debts and reorganize its operations. Following the foreclosure sale, the International-Great Northern Railroad Company was reorganized as the International & Great Northern Railway Company on December

31, 1922. This reorganization was intended to stabilize the company's finances and improve its operations.

The International-Great Northern Railroad Company faced several allegations of fraud throughout its history. One notable case was the issuance of bonds in 1871. The International Railroad Company issued $500,000 in bonds, signed by the governor and treasurer but not countersigned by the comptroller due to allegations of fraud in enacting the law. The Texas Supreme Court declared these bonds unconstitutional, highlighting the fraudulent practices involved.

Condition and Purposes of the International Railway Company.

The liabilities of the International Railway Company, in round numbers, amount to $18,000,000. It assets are 400 miles of road, the best in the South in all its facts and incidents, and worth $35,000 per mile, or $16,900,000. It owns 8600 shares, or 1,700,000 acres of the Texas land company's property, worth certainly $2,000,000. It owns, under the late act of the Legislature, for completed road, 2,611,280 acres of land. It owns 160,090 acres purchased for town sites, worth $1,000,000 or more, it is said. It owns 2863 shares of the Galveston, Houston and Henderson Railway; county $121,500, and city bonds $42,000. Estimating the railroad at anything like its cost, the company's assets are certainly at twenty-five per cent, greater value than the sum total of its liabilities. The largest bondholders of the company, Messrs. Sam Sloan, J. S. Kennedy, W. B. Dodge, P. M. Spofford, Moses Taylor, Thomas W. Pearsall, W. Walter Phelps, J. S. Wetmore, J. S. Barnes and W. M. Rice and others, agree to exchange over-due coupons for registered certificates of indebtedness, payable in gold, ten and fifteen years from date, with seven per cent. interest. The company have the right to redeem at any time, by giving ninety days' notice, any of these certificates of indebtedness. The holders of coupons of any of the bonds of the company should forward them at once to the office of the company, 52 Wall street.

Another significant case involving financial irregularities was United States v. Great Northern Railway Co. (1932). This case involved a payment made by the government to the International-Great Northern Railroad Company under the guaranty provision of the Transportation Act. The payment was not more than the amount due as certified by the Interstate Commerce Commission at the time, but it was later found to be an overpayment based on the Commission's final computation.

The court ruled that the discrepancy was due to using different formula for adjusting maintenance expenses and that the overpayment was not recoverable by the United States. These cases underscore the International-Great Northern Railroad Company's legal and ethical challenges, impacting on its reputation and operations.

Merger with Missouri Pacific Railroad (Mopac)

Several factors drove the Missouri Pacific Railroad (Mopac) merger in 1925. The International-Great Northern Railroad Company faced significant financial difficulties, entering receivership multiple times. The merger was a strategic move to stabilize the company's finances.

By merging, the International-Great Northern Railroad Company could benefit from Mopac's larger network and resources, improving operational efficiency and reducing costs. Additionally, the Gulf Coast Lines subsidiary, New Orleans, Texas, and Mexico Railway bought the International-Great Northern Railroad Company in 1924, and subsequently, Mopac acquired the Gulf Coast Lines in 1925. This was part of a planned corporate maneuver to keep the company within the Mopac fold. By March 1, 1956, the International-Great Northern Railroad Company was fully merged into the Missouri Pacific Railroad Company.

Merger with Union Pacific Railroad

The railroad industry saw significant consolidation in the mid-20th century to create more efficient and competitive entities. The merger of the Missouri Pacific Railroad into Union Pacific on September 11, 1997, was part of this broader trend. This merger allowed for the integration of the Missouri Pacific Railroad's (Mopac) network into a larger system, providing economic benefits through improved service and expanded reach. Union Pacific aimed to expand its network and services, and including the Missouri Pacific Railroad's (Mopac) routes helped achieve this goal, significantly impacting Texas's railway system.

THE

TEXARKANA GATEWAY

TO

TEXAS

AND THE

SOUTHWEST.

Fort Bend County, Texas,

HAS an area of 889 square miles, and a population of 12,000. Fort Bend County is in the second tier of counties from the Gulf. The Brazos River traverses the entire length of the county. The soil is deep alluvial, and very productive. Timber is mostly oak, pecan, walnut and cottonwood. The principal industries are sugar raising and farming. The International & Great Northern Railroad passes through the southeastern part of the county, and connecting at Arcola Junction with the Sugar Land Railway, and the Gulf, Colorado & Santa Fe Railway. The assessed value of property in 1894 was $5,114,080. Improved lands sell from $5 to $20 per acre; unimproved lands from $2 to $6 per acre. Average taxable value $5.42 per acre. The county rate of taxation is 65 cents on the $100. There are 44 mortgages, amounting to $44,215, on record; 380 farms are under cultivation, and 559 persons rent land for farming purposes. 546 farm laborers receive an average wage of $12.50 per month. Cotton is 50 per cent of the product, and sugar cane about 30 per cent, corn about 15 per cent, the balance made up of potatoes, peas, beans, broom corn and hay. There are 8,865 horses and mules, 52,519 cattle, 1,002 sheep, 4,515 hogs in the county.

BUSINESS. There are 50 mercantile establishments, 22 retail dealers, 1 ice factory, and several large sugar mills located in the county.

CHURCHES—The Baptist, Methodist, Episcopal, Christian and Catholic denominations are represented by fine churches.

Arcola, the principal town in the county, is located on the International & Great Northern Railroad,

Arcola Township
Early Development and Key Figures

In 1856, the Houston Tap and Brazoria Railway, soon nicknamed the *Sugar Road,* was chartered on September 1, with construction already underway by April 7; by October 21, trains were running between Houston and Pierce Junction. By 1858, the line crossed the Arcola Plantation, the vast sugar and cotton producing estate of Jonathan Dawson Waters, reached Sandy Point in 1859, and extended to East Columbia in 1860, passing through Hawdon and Juliff along the way. The Civil War in 1861 interrupted service as rails were removed for Confederate use, but the route's importance endured. In 1869, the Arcola Post Office opened beside the tracks at what is now FM 521 and Masterson, officially fixing the town's name on maps, schedules, and records, formally recognizing the community freed people had already established on former plantation land. By the late 1870s, added rail spurs secured the crossroads as a lasting transportation hub. These tracks were instrumental in the region's transportation and economic development.

The improved infrastructure attracted settlers and investors, fostering economic growth and population expansion. By 1884, the community had established a sugar mill, two steam-powered gristmills, cotton gins, two general stores, a Baptist church, and a school.

Arcola Township, a plantation town, blossomed into a vibrant community in the late 19th century, driven by influential figures such as Thomas William House Sr., William Walter Phelps, and Jonathan Dawson Waters. Their strategic vision and actions were pivotal in shaping the town's economic and infrastructural landscape during this time. In the mid-1840s, Jonathan Dawson Waters acquired a significant tract of land and established one of Texas's largest cotton and sugar plantations, naming it Arcola. The community later adopted this name, reflecting the plantation's importance in the region.

The Arcola Township area was originally part of the William Hall and David Fitzgerald Leagues, two of Austin's Old Three Hundred, enriching the early history of the region before being included in the I&GN Railroad and Manuel Escalero Surveys. Thomas William House Sr., a prominent businessman and owner of the Arcola Plantation, further contributed to the area's development. By integrating the railway with agricultural operations, he significantly boosted the local economy. The Gulf, Colorado, and Santa Fe Railway Station in Arcola became an essential stop, enhancing connectivity and trade and further contributing to the town's growth and prosperity.

William Walter Phelps played a pivotal role in the development of Arcola Township and Texas through his strategic land acquisitions and railroad investments. Driven by his growing passion for these ventures, he abandoned his law practice to fully dedicate himself to them. His work, particularly with the Manuel Escalero Survey in Arcola, was crucial in establishing the township's boundaries and fostering growth. However, despite his successes, Phelps's methods of land acquisition were not without controversy, leading to legal challenges that cast a shadow over his business practices.

The history of Arcola is deeply intertwined with the legacy of the enslaved individuals who contributed significantly to the growth and prosperity of Arcola Plantation. Their tireless labor and resilience laid the foundation for the community's existence. As time passed, their descendants continued this legacy, becoming the architects of the township of Arcola. Thanks to their unwavering dedication and commitment, Arcola has not only survived but flourished.

The Land Was Never Silent

The River Settlement

This chronicle charts how Black Texans, long denied land and liberty, reclaimed both through resilience, community building, and civic stewardship. The story begins not with ownership but with dispossession and traces a geography of resistance rooted in Abstracts 25, 31, 170, and 352.

Long before the name Arcola appeared on a federal map, there was the River Settlement communities of enslaved men, women, and children living and laboring along the Brazos near Bagdad Bend, Cedar Lake, and the lower reaches of the Judge Edward Palmer and Jonathan Waters Arcola Plantation. In bondage, families forged kinship, worshipped in brush arbors, and buried their dead in unmarked ground, holding together a lineage that freedom would later name.

Across the 1830s–1860s, sugarcane, cotton, and corn tied the River Settlement to the river and the plantations' fields and mills. Within this

world, people built family clusters and mutual care that would guide every move after emancipation.

Among those remembered from the River Settlement:

- Isaac *Ike* Johnson, an enslaved man on the Palmer place, who later carried the Gospel across Fort Bend and Galveston Counties.
- Mary Ann and Elijah Green, an enslaved couple near Bagdad Bend, whose children organized land purchases after the war.
- Sarah Jane *Miss Jane* McKinney, an enslaved midwife whose work linked river families to those who later settled near the junction.
- The Taylor and Washington families, enslaved kin networks with ties across multiple abstracts and overlapping labor on Palmer and Waters lands.

It is essential to acknowledge that influential figures such as Judge Edward Palmer and Jonathan Dawson Waters gained their wealth through the labor of enslaved people and would not have been able to turn Arcola into a vibrant community without them. Enslaved labor was the backbone of the plantation economy, driving the production of cotton and sugar, which were critical to the region's prosperity. The harsh conditions under which the enslaved people worked included long hours, grueling physical labor, and severe punishments. Despite these brutal conditions, the resilience and labor of the enslaved population were crucial in building the economic foundation of Arcola. Enslaved people were responsible for planting, tending, harvesting crops, and maintaining the plantation infrastructure. Their skills and knowledge in agriculture and craftsmanship were invaluable to the success of the plantations.

Therefore, these are not just names; they are the continuity of a people held in bondage who prepared, as best they could, for a different future.

Land, Law, and Legacy

In January 1865, as the Civil War staggered toward its close, Union General William T. Sherman issued *Special Field Orders No. 15,* a directive that promised to redistribute confiscated Confederate land to formerly enslaved families. The order applied only to coastal regions of South Carolina, Georgia, and parts of Florida. Texas was not included in this redistribution zone. Each eligible family was to receive up to forty acres, a profound, if fleeting, gesture of restitution.

Soon after, surplus army mules were issued to assist in cultivation, giving rise to the enduring phrase *forty acres and a mule.* This was not just symbolism; it was an attempt to create self-sufficiency and autonomy for people long denied both.

On April 14, 1865, President Abraham Lincoln's assassination shattered the fragile promise of land redistribution. His successor, Andrew Johnson, swiftly overturned Special Field Orders No. 15 and returned confiscated plantations to their former Confederate owners. Thousands of newly freed people, many of whom had cleared fields, built cabins, and began to cultivate the land, were now violently uprooted, dispossessed, and thrust into a new cycle of exploitation

This abrupt reversal deepened freed people's distrust of federal promises and set the stage for the next struggle over land rights.

The Galveston Daily News.

HOUSTON, WEDNESDAY, JUNE 21, 1865

HEADQUARTERS DISTRICT OF TEXAS, }
GALVESTON TEXAS, June 19, 1865. }

General Orders, No. 3.

The people are informed that, in accordance with a proclamation from the Executive of the United States, all slaves are free. This involves an absolute equality of personal rights and rights of property, between former masters and slaves, and the connection heretofore existing between them, becomes that between employer and hired labor.— The Freedmen are advised to remain at their present homes, and work for wages. They are informed that they will not be allowed to collect at military posts; and that they will not be supported in idleness either there or elsewhere.   By order of
Major-General GRANGER.

(Signed.)   F. W. EMERY, Maj. & A. A. G.

In Texas, Sherman's orders had never applied, so emancipation unfolded differently. On June 19, 1865, Union Major General Gordon Granger arrived in Galveston and issued General Order No. 3, proclaiming that all slaves were free. Although Arcola sat well inland, news of freedom spread rapidly along church networks and labor camps. There, formerly enslaved families gathered under brush arbors and beside riverbanks to pray, sing, and proclaim their liberty aloud. Many had long suspected the Confederacy's collapse but dared not celebrate until that clarion announcement. That afternoon did more than end bondage—it sparked land claims, inspired church building, and launched the civic organizing that would define Black Arcola's enduring legacy.

By December 1865, the Thirteenth Amendment formally abolished slavery, yet its exception clause permitting involuntary servitude as criminal punishment opened a legal back door for forced labor. Texas legislators raced to enact Black Codes that criminalized mundane behaviors like loitering, vagrancy, and alleged contract breaches.

As a result of these statutes, sham trials swept across the state. Throughout Texas, Black men were arrested en masse on trivial charges and then leased out to railroads, plantations, and mines. The state treasury and private companies profited handsomely while prisoners suffered beatings, starvation, and deadly labor camps. Although formal convict leasing ended in 1910, its brutal legacy endured through carceral farming and prison labor well into the twentieth century.

The federal government created the Freedmen's Bureau to assist formerly enslaved people, but in Texas, its power was limited. The Bureau negotiated labor contracts and offered short-term aid, yet it lacked the legal authority to allocate land. Unlike other Southern states, where the federal Southern Homestead Act of 1866 opened public land to freed people, Texas was explicitly excluded. Here, public land remained tightly controlled by the state, and racist market practices and governance made land acquisition nearly impossible for most. Instead, freed people were steered toward sharecropping and tenant farming systems that kept them in economic bondage.

INITIATION NEAR RICHMOND Tex

The Ku Klux Klan

The Ku Klux Klan (KKK) emerged as a significant threat to the Black community in Arcola and surrounding areas during the Reconstruction era and beyond. Founded in 1865, the KKK used terror and violence to intimidate and suppress Black citizens, aiming to maintain white supremacy and prevent Black people from exercising their newly gained rights. The presence of the KKK in Texas, including Fort Bend County, created an atmosphere of fear and oppression for the Black community. *Come on in, I'll show you something (going to another room). This is my daddy's KKK card. In 1900, 1915, something like that, they had this revolt out here, where these blacks, the ones doing all the planning, they actually started a shooting war over there. Every red blooded white man in Houston joined the KKK. I told my daddy, I said, "Daddy, why don't you tell me about it?" He said, "I wasn't very proud of it."* (Howard Grounds, Oral History 2007).

Jaybird Woodpecker War

The Jaybird Woodpecker War (1888–1889) was a violent and politically charged conflict between two US Democratic Party factions in Fort Bend County, Texas, that underscored the racial and political tensions of the post-Reconstruction South. This struggle pitted the Jaybirds, an all-white Democratic faction, against the Woodpeckers, a biracial coalition of Republicans that had dominated the county's

Democratic party and government since Reconstruction. The Jaybirds sought to reclaim control of the county government, culminating in the Battle of Richmond in 1889. Their victory resulted in the disenfranchisement of Black voters and the establishment of white supremacy in the region.

The Jaybirds' efforts to regain power extended beyond local support. White men from across the county rallied to their cause, reflecting a broader national commitment to restoring white dominance in the South during this period. During the Battle of Richmond, they received support from the Houston Light Guards, a state militia, the Texas Rangers, and Texas Governor Lawrence Ross. The governor played a pivotal role by mediating the conflict and ultimately placing the Jaybirds in charge of the county government after the removal of Woodpecker officials. This widespread support was instrumental in their success and led to the implementation of discriminatory practices, such as whites-only primaries, which excluded Black citizens from political participation for decades.

Following their victory, the Jaybird Democratic Association was formed in 1889, cementing 25 years of political dominance in Fort Bend County. Among its founding officers, F.M.O. Otis Fenn served as secretary, while his father, John R. Fenn, joined the Executive Committee alongside J.H.P. Davis and J.M. Moore. The Fenn family, based in Duke, Texas, played an active role in the local community, with John R. Fenn also serving as Duke's first Postmaster.

During this period, the Ku Klux Klan's presence further heightened racial tensions. Although not officially affiliated with the Jaybirds, the Klan's activities underscored the broader use of violence and intimidation to suppress Black political rights. The Jaybird Democratic Association operated within this racially charged climate, embodying the systemic hierarchies that defined the era. The Fenn family's involvement in these events reflects their alignment with the association's goals of consolidating white political power, illustrating how personal legacies intersect with the broader forces shaping the region's history.

Yet despite these constraints, Black Texans made a way out of no way. They bought land privately, when possible, sometimes through informal agreements and communal pooling. They built freedom colonies, Black settlements where land, memory, and kinship were intertwined. These communities, often relegated to flood-prone or bottomland areas rejected by white buyers, became sacred geographies of resistance. By 1910, about one-third of the state's farm operators were Black, though most were tenants rather than owners. Even so, their determination reshaped the landscape, both physically and spiritually.

After emancipation: Movement toward the rails (1865–1870s)

After the Civil War in 1865, newly Freedmen and Freedwomen (collectively, freed people) made deliberate choices. Some remained near the river, purchasing small plots or settling on church lands. Others moved inland toward the emerging rail corridor, seeking wage work, markets, schools, and the protection that proximity sometimes offered. Among these freed people were veterans of the United States Colored Troops, such as Isaac Green, John Taylor, Samuel Johnson, Henry Williams, and Thomas Brown, who had served with honor during the Civil War. These individuals made their way to Fort Bend County and settled within the land parcels now known as Abstracts 170, 352, 31, and 25. These were not just places of residence; they became the geographic backbone of Arcola's Black schools, churches, and cemeteries.

Their names appear in Freedmen's Bureau contracts, federal census rolls, tax ledgers, and oral histories. They cleared fields, raised families, petitioned for school land, and helped establish institutions that would serve generations. In 1869, the establishment of the Arcola Post Office near the rail lines at today's FM 521 and Masterson did two things at once: it formalized the name Arcola. It fixed the town's location on federal postal maps, railroad schedules, and county records. That administrative act recognized what freed people had already made a community and anchored it at the junction. By 1878, the addition of rail spurs had made the intersection a reliable transportation hub.

Freed people from the River Settlement, Greens, McKinneys, Taylors, and Washingtons re-rooted there, establishing homes, churches, and classrooms along Abstracts 25, 31, 170, and 352. It is the crossroads where river lineage met rail possibility and where a Black community claimed civic identity in its own name.

Abstract 25– The David Fitzgerald Survey

In 1824, David Fitzgerald, one of Stephen F. Austin's *Old Three Hundred* colonists, received a Mexican land grant that became Abstract 25 in Fort Bend County. This tract was part of Austin's first colony and represents one of the earliest surveyed parcels in Texas. Fitzgerald's grant established the legal foundation for what would later become the Arcola Plantation, a massive slaveholding operation under Jonathan Dawson Waters, who enslaved between 200–500 people.

The enslaved men, women, and children forced to labor here worked in cotton and sugar production. Sugar cultivation was especially brutal, with high mortality rates. After emancipation in 1865, many Freedmen families remained on the Fitzgerald Survey land. They leased or purchased parcels, built homes, founded churches, and educated their children. Their resilience transformed Abstract 25 from a plantation into a Freedmen Settlement.

Williams Family

Henry Williams (1842–1910) was enslaved on the Arcola Plantation within the Fitzgerald Survey. After emancipation, he became a farmer and leased 20 acres in Abstract 25. He was buried locally.

Sarah Williams (1848–1922), his wife, was a homemaker and joint landholder. She was baptized at Arcola Baptist Church.

James Williams (1875–1950), their son, became a teacher. His children were listed in the 1903 Arcola school rosters, confirming the family's educational legacy.

Johnson Family

Samuel Johnson (1838–1905) was enslaved on the Arcola Plantation. After emancipation, he became a farmer and leased 15 acres in Abstract 25, as recorded in deed books in 1878. He also served as a deacon at Arcola Baptist Church.

Mary Johnson (1845–1912), his wife, was a homemaker and joint landholder. She was buried locally.

John Johnson (1872–1948), their son, worked as a laborer and tenant farmer. His children were enrolled in Arcola schools.

Sarah Johnson (1878–1955), their daughter, became a teacher and was documented in Arcola ISD rosters.

Brown Family

Thomas Brown (c.1840–1902) was enslaved on the Arcola Plantation. After emancipation, he worked in the sugar mill and leased land in Abstract 25 during the 1880s (acreage not specified). He was buried in the Riceton–Arcola Cemetery.

Eliza Brown (c.1847–1915), his wife, was a homemaker and joint landholder. She was baptized at Arcola Baptist Church.

William Brown (1874–1951), their son, became a farmer and tenant farmer in Abstract 25. His children were enrolled in Arcola schools.

Washington Family

George Washington (c.1835–1900) was enslaved on the Arcola Plantation. After emancipation, he became a farmer and civic leader. He owned a small parcel in Abstract 25 (acreage not specified) and was remembered in oral histories for his leadership.

Martha Washington (c.1842–1918), his wife, was a homemaker and joint landholder. She was buried in the Riceton–Arcola Cemetery.

Henry Washington (1870–1945), their son, became a teacher. He did not own land but was listed in Arcola school records.

Smith Family

Isaac Smith (c.1839–1907) was enslaved on the Arcola Plantation. After emancipation, he became a farmer and leased parcels in Abstract 25 (acreage not specified). He was buried in the Riceton–Arcola Cemetery.

Anna Smith (c.1846–1910), his wife, was a homemaker and joint landholder. She was active in Arcola Baptist Church.

James Smith (1878–1956), their son, worked as a laborer and tenant farmer. His children were enrolled in Arcola schools.

Robinson Family

Peter Robinson (c.1843–1908) was enslaved on the Arcola Plantation. After emancipation, he became a farmer and leased parcels in Abstract 25 (acreage not specified). He was buried in the Riceton–Arcola Cemetery.

Clara Robinson (c.1850–1915), his wife, was a homemaker and joint landholder. She was baptized at Arcola Baptist Church.

Samuel Robinson (1876–1952), their son, worked as a laborer and tenant farmer. His children were listed in Arcola schools.

Jackson Family

David Jackson (c.1841–1903) was enslaved on the Arcola Plantation. After emancipation, he became a farmer and leased parcels in Abstract 25 (acreage not specified). He was buried in the Riceton–Arcola Cemetery.

Mary Jackson (c.1849–1917), his wife, was a homemaker and joint landholder. Church records confirm her baptisms at Arcola Baptist.

John Jackson (1879–1954), their son, worked as a laborer and tenant farmer. His children were enrolled in Arcola schools.

Carter Family

Nathan Carter (c.1837–1906) was enslaved on the Arcola Plantation. After emancipation, he became a farmer. Tax rolls confirm his land use in Abstract 25 (acreage not specified). He was buried in the Riceton–Arcola Cemetery.

Sarah Carter (c.1844–1914), his wife, was a homemaker and joint landholder. She was baptized at Arcola Baptist Church.

Joseph Carter (1875–1950), their son, worked as a laborer and tenant farmer. His children were listed in Arcola schools.

Taylor Family

William Taylor (c.1840–1905) was enslaved on the Arcola Plantation. After emancipation, he became a farmer. Deed records tie him to

Abstract 25 (acreage not specified). He was buried in the Riceton–Arcola Cemetery.

Hannah Taylor (c.1848–1916), his wife, was a homemaker and joint landholder. She was baptized at Arcola Baptist Church.

Robert Taylor (1877–1953), their son, became a teacher. He did not own land but was documented in Arcola school records.

Green Family

Charles Green (c.1836–1904) was enslaved on the Arcola Plantation. After emancipation, he became a farmer. Abstract 25 transactions list the Greens as landholders (acreage not specified). He was buried in the Riceton–Arcola Cemetery.

Lucy Green (c.1843–1911), his wife, was a homemaker and joint landholder. She was baptized at Arcola Baptist Church.

Edward Green (1879–1957), their son, worked as a laborer and tenant farmer. His children were enrolled in Arcola schools.

Community Anchors

Arcola Baptist Church: Built inside Abstract 25 on the east side of FM 521, this was the first organized Black congregation in Arcola after emancipation. It served as a spiritual anchor, a schoolhouse, and a civic hub.

Education: By 1903, Arcola's Black schools enrolled 176 pupils, many from these families. Teachers from the Williams, Johnson, Washington, and Taylor families contributed to education.

Burials: Families were buried in local plots within Abstract 25 and in the Riceton–Arcola Cemetery.

Occupations: Farming, tenant labor, sugar mill work, teaching, and church leadership defined the Freedmen community's livelihood.

Legacy

The families of Abstract 25, Williams, Johnson, Brown, Washington, Smith, Robinson, Jackson, Carter, Taylor, and Green were enslaved on the Arcola Plantation before 1865. After emancipation, they became the foundation of Arcola's Freedmen community. They leased or purchased land (with acreage documented for Williams and Johnson), built churches, educated their children, and buried their loved ones in local cemeteries. Their descendants remain in Fort Bend County today, tied to churches, civic groups, and oral traditions.

Abstract 25, rooted in David Fitzgerald's 1824 Austin Colony grant, stands as a living archive of Texas history, from colonization, through slavery, to freedom and community resilience.

Abstract 31 – The William Hall Survey and Palestine Baptist Church

Amid these grand transactions and political maneuvers, Abstract 31 tells a different story, one of community emergence after the trauma of slavery. Located within the William Hall Survey, this abstract became a sanctuary for formerly enslaved families. The founding of Palestine Baptist Church in 1870 marked not just a spiritual beginning but a civic declaration: these people, denied citizenship, freedom, and access to land for generations, were now carving out a self-determined future.

Legal documents in the Fort Bend County Clerk's Office trace land purchases dating back to the 1870s. Deeds, surveys, and plat maps show how freed families slowly accumulated parcels, built homes, and established institutions that anchored their freedom in law. A 1943 deed confirms the church's location within the William Hall League, underscoring its role as both a spiritual heart and geographic anchor.

What unfolded in Abstract 31 was a quiet revolution. Landownership here was not merely about acreage, it was about autonomy. Residents founded schools, formed burial societies, and created networks of mutual support. As generations passed, the children of these founders moved into skilled labor, education, ministry, and civic leadership. Their legacies endured, not only through careers but in the continuation of churches, cemeteries, and homes whose roots reach back to emancipation.

Between 1870 and 1900, the William Hall Survey was home to several formerly enslaved families who became landowners and community builders. Henry Jackson, born around 1825 and formerly enslaved, worked as a farmer and acquired 30 acres in 1878. He lived with his wife Martha, a housekeeper, and their children Sarah, a domestic worker, and John, who had no listed occupation. John later became a farmer and acquired 60 acres in 1920, living with his wife Mary and their children Tom, Helen, and Fred.

Samuel Turner, born circa 1820 and formerly enslaved, labored as a sharecropper and farmer alongside his wife, Eliza. Their children included Joseph, a farmhand, and Lucy, a student. Lucy later became Lucy Turner Carter, a widow who purchased 25 acres in 1934 and lived with her son, Simon, a student.

Louisa Williams, a laundry worker born around 1822, purchased 10 acres in 1895 after the death of her husband George in 1893. She raised two children, Rachel and Isaac, both students. Rachel later became Rachel Williams Smith, a teacher who inherited 80 acres in 1938. She lived with her husband Joseph and their daughter Alice.

Also residing in the William Hall Survey were Henry Green (b. 1845), formerly enslaved on the Hall estate, and his wife, Louisa Green (b. 1850). They purchased 40 acres in 1878 and raised Sarah (b. 1871), a seamstress; Henry Jr. (b. 1873), a railroad laborer; and Mary (b. 1875), a homemaker. Henry Green served as a trustee at Palestine Baptist Church.

Isaac Taylor (b. 1838), formerly enslaved, purchased 60 acres in 1882. He and his wife, Mary (b. 1842), raised James (b. 1866), a schoolteacher and church clerk; Eliza (b. 1868), a midwife; and Isaac Jr. (b. 1870), a farm laborer.

John Jackson (b. 1840) and Matilda Jackson (b. 1845) acquired 50 acres in 1879. Their children, William (b. 1867) and Clara (b. 1870), continued the family's civic and religious engagement, William as a deacon and farmer, Clara through marriage into the Brown family. Jackson himself was a deacon at Palestine Baptist.

George Williams (b. 1855), born free, purchased 30 acres in 1885. He and Emma Williams (b. 1860) had two children: George Jr. (b. 1880), who worked as a railroad switchman, and Lucy (b. 1882), who became a teacher and married Joseph Evans Jr. of Abstract 170.

Elijah Robinson (b. 1852) and Sarah Robinson (b. 1856) acquired 25 acres in 1881. Their children, Elijah Jr. (b. 1878) and Ruth (b. 1880), both entered education, Elijah Jr. as a teacher and Ruth as a church pianist and domestic worker.

Moses Johnson (b. 1835), formerly enslaved, purchased 40 acres in 1880. He and Eliza Johnson (b. 1840) raised Thomas (b. 1865), who became a railroad foreman, and Rachel (b. 1868), who married into the Stewart family of Abstract 352.

Peter Washington (b. 1848) and Lucy Washington (b. 1852) acquired 35 acres in 1883. Their children, Peter Jr. (b. 1875) and Anna (b. 1877), continued in agriculture and domestic work, with Anna marrying into the Coleman family.

Thomas Brown (b. 1830), formerly enslaved, purchased 45 acres in 1877. He and Rebecca Brown (b. 1835) raised Clara (b. 1858), who married into the Jackson family, and Thomas Jr. (b. 1860), a Baptist preacher. The Browns were active in Palestine Baptist, with Clara noted for her church involvement.

These families were deeply connected to Palestine Baptist Church, founded in 1870. The church remains active today at 4200 FM 521 Road in Arcola.

1839 Fort Bend Map

Abstract 170 – The Manuel Escalero Survey

The history of Abstract 170 in Fort Bend County begins with Manuel Escalero, a Mexican-born soldier whose name is etched into the early military story of Texas. Born and raised in Béxar County, Escalero enlisted in the Texas Army on June 7, 1835, serving under Captain Juan Seguín and later Captain Antonio Menchaca through 1837. He fought in key battles of the Texas Revolution, including the Siege of Béxar, where Texian forces ousted Mexican troops from San Antonio. He later participated in frontier expeditions against Indigenous tribes and, during a campaign at Lost Lake, was captured and imprisoned in Matamoros, Mexico. Enduring hunger, overcrowding, and disease, Escalero escaped captivity in 1839 and returned to Texas. His military service earned him substantial land rights. On November 2, 1853, Escalero purchased 1,280 acres from John C. French. A year later, he was awarded a bounty warrant for another 1,280 acres; subsequently, he received an additional 320-acre bounty and a 640-acre donation.

These grants, registered in 1858 and formally approved in 1859, brought his holdings to over 3,500 acres. His land, surveyed by L. Colquhoun in 1847, neighbored David Fitzgerald, Thomas Barnett, and William Hall Leagues. Though Black and Native peoples were explicitly denied land grants under Republic-era law, confirmed by the Texas Constitution, Escalero's service and ethnicity positioned him within an exempted group, reflecting how Texas stratified racial access to land even before formal statehood.

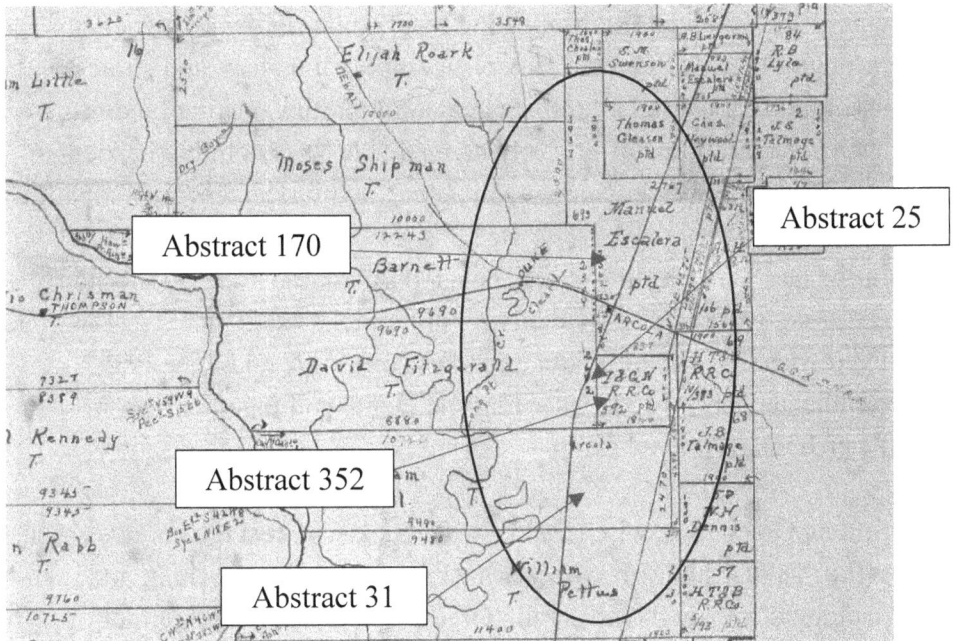

Two decades later, Escalero's legacy became part of a broader land-transfer trend. On March 28, 1872, surveyor L. Colquhoun appeared before a Bexar County court to affirm his legal role in the Escalero Survey. This affidavit enabled financier William Walter Phelps of New Jersey to acquire the land. On January 10, 1874, Phelps purchased 3,129.25 acres, two-thirds of a league and one labor, for $1,251.60 in gold from L. Colquhoun. That same year, a corrected survey reduced the total acreage to about 14.5 million square varas (from 15.56 million), refining the survey's boundaries. In 1878, the International &

Great Northern Railroad was granted 576 acres, leaving 2,942.96 acres under Phelps's control. He later transferred this land to the New York & Texas Land Company in 1889, a corporation he helped establish to broker and sell vast tracts of Texas land.

While Phelps served as a U.S. Congressman and later as Minister to Germany, he was also a key player in speculative land development. His acquisition of the Escalero Survey exemplifies how former bounty lands were incorporated into national portfolios and commercial enterprises, effectively disentitling local communities to ownership through the use of layered surveys, complex transfers, and strategic speculation. For Black families and communities seeking land nearby, such concentrations of property created near-impenetrable barriers to ownership. However, some were able to acquire land against all odds.

In the late 19th century, Peter Harris, born around 1830 and formerly enslaved, worked as a field laborer and purchased 20 acres in 1881. He lived with his wife Margaret and their sons Isaac and Pete, both farmhands. Isaac Harris later married Delia, and together they raised Peter Jr. and Tilda.

Sophia Green, born circa 1835, was a cook who received 5 acres as a gift in 1890. She lived with her husband Moses, a carpenter, and their daughters Julia and Anna. Julia Green Williams, granddaughter of Sophia, inherited 4 acres in 1944. She lived with her husband, Edwin, and their daughters Pearl and Sonia.

Charles Ross (b. 1844), a freedman and church trustee, purchased 50 acres in 1886. With his wife Nancy (b. 1848), he raised Charles Jr. (b. 1870), a civic organizer and land broker, and Ella (b. 1872), a homemaker.

James Grice (b. 1850) and Martha Grice (b. 1853) acquired 40 acres in 1888. Their son Henry (b. 1875) became a teacher, while their daughter Lillian (b. 1877) worked as a domestic laborer.

Henry Davis (b. 1842), formerly enslaved, purchased 35 acres in 1881. His children, Isaac (b. 1865) and Mary (b. 1868), worked as farm labor and a cook, respectively.

Isaac Coleman (b. 1855) acquired 30 acres in 1889. His children, Samuel (b. 1880) and Anna (b. 1882) became a teacher and a homemaker. Anna later married into the Washington family of Abstract 31.

William Harris (b. 1840), formerly enslaved, purchased 40 acres in 1882. His children, George (b. 1865) and Lucy (b. 1867), worked in the railroad and as a seamstress.

George Lee (b. 1858) and Mary Lee (b. 1860) acquired 25 acres in 1890. Their children, John (b. 1880) and Clara (b. 1883) entered civic and educational roles.

Benjamin Scott (b. 1836), formerly enslaved, purchased 50 acres in 1878. His children, Benjamin Jr. (b. 1865) and Ruth (b. 1867) became farmers and teachers.

Joseph Evans (b. 1845) acquired 30 acres in 1883. His son Joseph Jr. (b. 1870) married Lucy Williams of Abstract 31 and continued farming; daughter Sarah (b. 1872) was a homemaker.

Samuel Thomas (b. 1839), formerly enslaved, purchased 45 acres in 1879. His children, Thomas Jr. (b. 1865) and Eliza (b. 1868) became a Baptist preacher and a cook.

By the early 20th century, Pete Harris, son of Peter and Margaret, became a farmer and acquired 38 acres in 1922. He lived with his wife Alma and their children Lillian, a teacher; David, a farm laborer; and Eva, a student. Lillian Harris Wright, daughter of Pete, received 2 acres as a dowry in 1940.

Abstract 352 – I&GN Railroad Corridor

Minnequa Gardens | St. Paul AME Church (Historic)

The story of Abstract 352 is tethered to Texas's infrastructure boom and its speculative underside. In 1870, Phelps joined the board of the International Railroad Company, which merged three years later with the Houston & Great Northern Railroad to form the International & Great Northern Railroad (I&GN). Its goal was to build a railway from the Red River to Laredo and expand into Mexico. By 1876, the tracks reached Austin, San Antonio by 1880, and Laredo by 1881. In 1879, the Texas Legislature passed the Fifty Cent Act, allowing public land sales at fifty cents per acre, half the revenue earmarked for debt retirement and half for a school fund. This act opened 52 counties in West Texas, and over three million acres were sold. But widespread fraud and speculative abuse led to its repeal in 1883.

Though originally surveyed for railroad use, Abstract 352 evolved with the growth of private development. By the 1950s, it had entered private hands, and developers platted Minnequa Gardens, a residential subdivision with mapped streets and legal filings lodged in Fort Bend County. A 2021 legal notice confirmed the existence and boundaries of Lot One in Minnequa Gardens, solidifying its place within Abstract 352 and the public record.

Here again, land originally envisioned for infrastructure served another economic purpose. It became the site of generational homes, but its origins, from railroad charters and speculative surveys, highlight the entangled layers through which Black communities had to maneuver to achieve landholding in Fort Bend County.

Joshua Brown, born around 1830 and formerly enslaved, worked as a railroad laborer and lived on company land with his wife, Matilda, and their children James and Emma. By the early 20th century, James Brown, son of Joshua and Matilda, became a train porter and purchased 5 acres in 1925. He lived with his wife, Ella, and their sons Will and Samuel. Emma Brown Taylor, daughter of Joshua and Matilda, became a teacher and inherited 12 acres in 1930. She lived with her husband Charles and their son Lawrence.

Isaac Reed, born circa 1825 and formerly enslaved, served as a section foreman and lived in company housing with his wife, Harriet, and their son Moses. Moses Reed, son of Isaac and Harriet, worked as a warehouse laborer and leased 10 acres in 1942. He lived with his wife Dora and their daughter Ida, a factory worker.

Annie Pollard, a cook born around 1820 and formerly enslaved, lived as a tenant with her daughter, Laura. No land ownership is recorded, but Annie's household was listed in early tenant rolls for the railroad corridor.

Also residing in the I&GN corridor were several families who transitioned from railroad employment to land ownership:

- David Stewart (b. 1850), a Freedman, leased land from the railroad in 1885. His children, Rachel (b. 1875) and David Jr. (b. 1877) entered domestic work and railroad labor. Rachel married into the Johnson family of Abstract 31.
- Henry Moore (b. 1857) purchased 30 acres in 1887. His children, Henry Jr. (b. 1880) and Clara (b. 1882) became a teacher and a seamstress.
- John Clark (b. 1845), formerly enslaved, acquired 40 acres in 1880. His children, John Jr. (b. 1870) and Mary (b. 1872) became a farmer and a teacher. Clark served as a deacon in the local church.
- Isaac Nelson (b. 1852) purchased 35 acres in 1886. His children, Isaac Jr. (b. 1875) and Anna (b. 1878), worked in farming and domestic labor.
- Jacob Reed (b. 1838), formerly enslaved, acquired 45 acres in 1878. His children, Jacob Jr. (b. 1865) and Ruth (b. 1867) became a farmer and a church organist.
- Andrew Mitchell (b. 1855) purchased 30 acres in 1889. His children, Andrew Jr. (b. 1882) and Clara (b. 1884) became a teacher and a homemaker.
- Thomas Fisher (b. 1840), formerly enslaved, acquired 40 acres in 1882. His children, Thomas Jr. (b. 1865) and Eliza (b. 1868), worked as laborers and cooks.
- William Owens (b. 1850) purchased 35 acres in 1884. His children, William Jr. (b. 1875) and Lucy (b. 1877) continued farming and domestic work.
- Elijah Banks (b. 1843) acquired 30 acres in 1881. His children, Elijah Jr. (b. 1868) and Sarah (b. 1870) became a teacher and a homemaker.

These families were associated with St. Paul AME Church, founded around 1885. Though no longer active in Arcola, the closest AME congregation is located at 1554 Gears Road in Houston.

Arcola Farms and Minnequa Gardens

The landscapes of Abstract 170 and Abstract 352 would again transform during the Great Depression and postwar decades, reflecting both the endurance of Black settlement and the pressures of expanding development in Fort Bend County. These parcels, once tied to military service, speculative railroad expansion, and exclusionary land policy, became the stage for community-driven survival and reinvention.

On May 22, 1935, as economic hardship gripped the nation, a portion of Abstract 170 the Manuel Escalero Survey was platted into Arcola Farms, a 290.25-acre subdivision in the southern reach of Escalero's original holdings. The plat, filed officially with the Fort Bend County Clerk on July 9, 1935, was surveyed by Arthur H. Jungman and J. Frank Thompson. Though conceived as a formal subdivision, Arcola Farms became more than a mapped grid—it evolved into a vibrant settlement of formerly enslaved families and their descendants. These families, many of whom had labored nearby or inherited land informally, expanded their presence across the International & Great Northern Railroad and Manuel Escalero Surveys. Together, they built homes, cultivated gardens, founded institutions, and forged a tight-knit network rooted in shared memory and communal resilience.

The formation of Arcola Farms is significant not only for its geography but for its timing. In the 1930s, federal programs like the New Deal largely bypassed rural Black communities in Texas, and segregation remained a barrier to infrastructure, housing, and social services. Against these odds, Black families in Arcola staked a claim to the land, transforming legal parcels into spiritual homeplaces. What had once been bounty land for a Mexican veteran of Texas independence was now shaped by Black hands and sacred intention. Churches, schools, and family cemeteries emerged, tying past to present across legal boundaries and bloodlines.

A generation later, Abstract 352, the former International & Great Northern Railroad Survey, entered a new chapter. The rise of automobiles and the development of the Interstate Highway System in the 1950s reduced reliance on railroads, resulting in decreased rail traffic and the eventual decline of the Gulf, Colorado, and Santa Fe Railway, as well as the Houston Tap and Brazoria Railway. Economic downturns, including the Great Depression, further impacted the railroad industry, resulting in reduced investment and maintenance. The closure of railway stations in Arcola severely affected the community, which had depended on railroads for its economic growth and connectivity.

As a result, developers moved to subdivide portions of this once-railroad-affiliated tract. The outcome was Minnequa Gardens, a residential community formally mapped and filed with the Fort Bend County Clerk's Office. Streets were carved out, lots were defined, and easements recorded, bringing Abstract 352 fully into the domain of private ownership and civic mapping. The railroad survey that once cut across the state with economic ambition was now being parceled into homes, each holding a story of movement from enslavement to agency, from speculation to settlement.

Survival and Adaptation

The decline of railroads and the challenges faced by the plantation marked a significant turning point for Arcola Township. The loss of these critical economic drivers resulted in a population decrease, as many residents moved away in search of better opportunities. Despite these setbacks, Arcola Township managed to survive and adapt over the years, thanks to the descendants of the enslaved individuals who created self-sufficient communities with distinctive architecture, schools, and places of worship within Abstracts 25, 31, 170, and 352. By preserving the cultural and historical heritage passed down through generations, their efforts ensured that the community remained strong and vibrant.

Their pivotal role in Arcola Township's development and survival is a story of strength, perseverance, and an indomitable spirit that continues to inspire and shape the future of Arcola.

City of Arcola

Arcola, located in the vibrant Fort Bend County, offers a unique blend of rural charm and urban convenience. With a reputation for its strong sense of community and progressive vision, Arcola is a town where rich traditions pave the way for new opportunities.

As the township's population grew to 680 residents, community leaders recognized the need for formal governance and essential services. On December 17, 1980, a group of 20 devoted community members submitted an application to Fort Bend County Judge Jodie E. Stavinoha, aiming to officially incorporate Arcola as a Town. The proposed incorporation area encompassed exactly two miles.

After a thorough review, Judge Stavinoha determined the application met Texas laws for incorporation, which required a population between 225 and 2,000 residents. She ordered a Special Election of Incorporation to take place on January 17, 1981, at the Jake Dove Community Center. Voting hours were set from 7:00 AM to 7:00 PM. Mike Saenz was appointed to preside over the election, with authority to select two judges and two clerks to assist in managing the event. On January 17, 1981, registered voters from the unincorporated Town of Arcola convened at the Jake Dove Community Center to cast their votes in the Special Incorporation Election. The results demonstrated overwhelming support for incorporation, with 101 votes in favor and only 10 against. Mike Saenz oversaw the election with assistance from Election Judges Johnny Lee Cooper and Odell Sessum, as well as Election Clerks Susie Saenz and Harry W. Keryam. Fort Bend County Judge Jodie E. Stavinoha officially certified the election results on January 19, 1981.

On May 18, 1981, city officials unanimously voted 5–0 to formally designate Arcola as a city. This landmark decision, enshrined in Ordinance No. 5, marked a significant step in the township's transformation into a city.

Mike R. Saenz, Mayor
Carolyn Sessum, Alderwoman
Ronald McCann, Alderman
Carol Kingsbury, Alderman
Johnny R. Deleon, Alderman
Reverend Johnny L. Cooper, Alderman
City Secretary Susie Saenz
Adoption Vote: Yes: 5 No: 0

However, there are no documented records of elections specifically for Mike Saenz being elected as Mayor of Arcola or for the town's council members. It is likely that leadership roles during Arcola's early incorporation were informally assigned or established through undocumented processes.

In 1982, Arcola adopted a Type A City Charter, formalizing its governance structure and expanding its municipal authority. The city's origins were humble: it began with a rummage sale, and its City Hall was housed in a beer joint. That improvisational foundation set the stage for a governance dispute in 1984, when Mayor Mike Saenz was locked out of the municipal building by William Tripp, the property owner and Saenz's brother-in-law. The city claimed it had paid $1,914.21 in rent and invested $4,000 in renovations in lieu of further rental payments. Tripp, however, asserted that the city owed him $4,000 in rent. As tensions escalated, city officials vacated the building, and someone ripped a panel off the wall. City records were relocated to Mayor Saenz's home. City Attorney Steve Gilbert explained the move was driven by fear of being locked out entirely. The police department, also displaced, operated out of patrol cars. The city council continued its operations by holding meetings in a parking lot. The episode underscores the fragility of municipal infrastructure when personal ties, informal origins, and public accountability collide.

In 1986, Arcola implemented a Council-Manager form of government. The City Council, serving as the legislative body, plays a crucial role in shaping the city's future by making key decisions regarding policies, budgets, and development projects. Incorporation allowed Arcola to establish a local government capable of addressing the needs of its growing population more efficiently. This formal governance structure has significantly improved the city's planning and resource management.

The council comprises a mayor and five council members, all elected at large. They are responsible for appointing a City Administrator, who oversees the daily operations of the city government and has the authority to approve and manage personnel policies. The mayor and council members work closely with the City Administrator to plan for sustainable growth, improve infrastructure, and enhance the quality of life for residents. This structure helps ensure efficient management and responsiveness to the community's needs.

On March 7, 1987, the City of Arcola marked an important milestone with the grand opening and ribbon-cutting ceremony of its new 15,000 square foot City Hall building, located at 13222 Highway 6. This $269,000 project stood as a symbol of progress for the city. The ceremony, led by Mayor Mike Saenz and City Council members Ora Lee Tribble, Linda Carranza, Gloria Washington, Marjorie Pickett, and Alvin Gipson, was a proud moment for the community. Steve Gilbert served as the Master of Ceremonies, while guest speakers Carlos Colina Vargas and Charles Michulka brought inspiring words to the event.

Just two years later, in April 1989, the city received substantial financial backing to address its wastewater management system. The Texas Water Development Board invested $325,000 through certificates of obligation, while the U.S. Environmental Protection Agency awarded a grant of $957,962. The Texas Department of Commerce contributed $775,000 in 1991, followed by an additional $195,000 purchase of certificates by the Water Development Board. To secure these funds, the city passed ordinances that mandated the creation of a special fund for certificate payments, the levying of a tax to support this fund, and the segregation of wastewater system revenue from other city funds. These measures underscored the city's commitment to improving its infrastructure, yet significant challenges lay ahead.

Despite the financial investment, the resulting sanitary sewer system, constructed with over $2 million in federal grant money, fell short of compliance with state design criteria. Furthermore, inspection records and documentation of change orders were incomplete and unclear. As a result, the Texas Water Development Board could not recognize the system as complete, leaving the city at risk of facing a lien for the full grant amount until necessary corrections were made to meet state standards.

By 1992, the situation had escalated. Auditors from the Texas Water Development Board conducted over 30 visits to Arcola to assist with bookkeeping and requested financial records related to the wastewater system. However, the city's repeated failure to comply prompted the State of Texas to intervene. A lawsuit was filed in the Travis County District Court to compel the city to provide the necessary financial documentation, account for revenues and expenses, and implement proper billing for wastewater services.

The gravity of the situation was further highlighted when Attorney General Dan Morales sought the appointment of a temporary receiver to manage the city's financial matters. This led to the appointment of AM-TEX Corporation as temporary receiver on January 23, 1993, marking a turning point in the city's efforts to regain control and compliance.

During a special meeting on August 10, 1993, the City of Arcola's council voted unanimously to remove Mayor Mike Saenz from his positions as municipal court judge and city administrator. An injunction was filed against Mike and Susie Saenz, barring them from taking any action against the city and requesting records he may have since an FBI investigation was underway (City Council Meeting, March 1, 1994). As a result, Mayor Pro Tem Linda Deleon took the helm of Arcola's city leadership.

AM-TEX Corporation was appointed as the new city administrator. To address administrative and financial issues, the receiver AM-TEX hired several firms: Roseman & Wiseman to handle delinquent tax matters, Stu Levin as the receiver's lawyer, Roland, Fry & Company for bookkeeping, McCall & Company to finalize the 1992 audit, and Tax Tech to review tax rolls and prepare the 1993 taxes. According to Butch Callegari, the city council has no authority to do anything under receivership.

During this meeting, Mr. Murray, a subcontractor from Uticon, addressed residents who were experiencing issues with the sewer lines connected to their homes. He stated that his company had installed the house lines, which were inspected and approved by the city's engineer. Murphy used the fact that the lines were inspected and approved by the city's engineer as a defense for the residents' issues with the system, offering no relief or solution to those suffering from raw sewage backup in their homes.

AM-TEX was eventually removed as Arcola's receiver on April 5, 1994, after an eight-month delay caused by their failure to address critical issues. Robert Hebert was appointed as the new receiver by the state attorney general. Upon his arrival, Hebert discovered that the city was in financial ruin, with AM-TEX claiming $1.2 million in debts, despite having generated $3.5 million in revenue through sales and property taxes between 1989 and 1993. Shockingly, although the city had several bank accounts, only about $30,000 in cash was available. The city was in disarray. The police department had been eliminated, the file cabinets were empty, and important records were found haphazardly stored in cardboard boxes. The municipal court was operating in a three-sided 15,000-square-foot unfinished municipal building, handling wastewater calls and billing for the water system mandated by the state.

One of Hebert's key findings was that the city council had ceased meeting regularly and had been excluded from the governance process. The tax rate was $1.26 per $100 of property valuation. The city faced claims exceeding $1.3 million; receiver AM-TEX before April 5, 1994, $164,950; Uticon $379,000; Mr. and Mrs. Saenz $190,000; TWOB debt service $47,000 per year; IRS $272.

Hebert's leadership brought immediate and transformative changes to the city. One of his first actions was to ensure that council meetings were held regularly and that the election process was properly followed. On May 7, 1994, Linda DeLeon made history by becoming Arcola's first female mayor, serving until May 4, 1996. Although the city remained under receivership, with formal administrative authority resting in the hands of the court-appointed receiver, DeLeon's election represented a breakthrough in civic trust and public representation.

As mayor, DeLeon worked closely with Receiver Robert Hebert, county officials, and residents to stabilize the city. Her leadership guaranteed that Arcola's citizens had both a voice and a visible advocate during a time when local authority was otherwise limited.

Acting on Hebert's recommendations, Travis County Judge Jeanne Meurer reduced the property tax rate from $1.26 to $1.00 per $100 valuation and lowered the city's debt to $850,000, which included $450,000 owed to the Texas Water Department. These actions marked a pivotal turning point in addressing Arcola's administrative and financial challenges.

In addition, Hebert sought to negotiate an interlocal agreement with the County Judge and Commissioner to assume responsibility for maintenance and building improvements. During this process, he discovered that the city did not actually own the property where its city hall was located. Undeterred, Hebert successfully secured the title to the property and then reinitiated negotiations with the county, ensuring that Arcola could move forward with stability and legitimacy.

On May 4, 1996, Abraham Jones was elected mayor of Arcola, a general-law municipality. The Arcola City Councilmembers voted unanimously on September 3, 1996, to remove Jones as mayor on the grounds of violating the city's waste discharge ordinance and appointed Councilmember Gipson as the new mayor. Jones contested this removal, arguing that the Council exceeded its authority. Jones filed a lawsuit, *Abraham Jones v. City of Arcola, Texas, Robert E. Hebert, Receiver for the City of Arcola, and City Council for the City of Arcola,* against the City of Arcola, the receiver Robert E. Hebert, and the City Council, seeking to have the removal proceedings declared null and void. However, the district court denied Jones's request for declaratory relief, and the Texas Court of Appeals affirmed the district court's judgment on July 29, 1999. This legal battle was part of the broader issues that led to the receivership of Arcola, which aimed at addressing financial mismanagement and restoring proper governance.

In February 1996, Johnson Development Corporation entered into a joint development agreement with AFG Pacific Properties, Inc. and Thompson Lake Partners, LTD. This agreement was to develop approximately 7,500 acres of land within the City's extraterritorial jurisdiction before its annexation. As a result, the City of Arcola annexed 196 acres within its Extra Territorial Jurisdiction on November 5, 1996. This area became part of Sienna Plantation, which was later annexed into Missouri City. The developer, AFG Pacific Properties, Inc., aimed to create a master-planned community covering approximately 7,500 acres in Fort Bend County and preferred that the entire project be located within Missouri City. To support this initiative, the developer paid $75,000 to the Texas Department of Transportation. This payment was designated for Arcola to cover its share of the right-of-way acquisition costs for widening two segments of State Highway 6. At that time, the City of Arcola was under receivership by the District Court of Travis County, Texas, and lacked the funds to cover the acquisition costs.

On January 8, 2002, the City of Arcola concluded its receivership. Robert Hebert delivered deposit slips totaling $528,435 in unencumbered funds to Mayor Roy Jackson. The judge's decision to allocate $402,152.13 to the general fund and $126,283.16 to the sewer enterprise fund significantly restored the city's financial stability.

This marked a major milestone for Arcola, indicating that the city had progressed enough to regain control over its management. The city could now focus on growth and development with improved governance structures. This transition also allowed Arcola to establish a new depository, ensuring the continuation of essential services and supporting further community development.

Councilmember Evelyn Jones, Mayor Pro Tem Ebony Sanco, Mayor Veeda Williams, Councilmember Greg Abarr, Councilmember Rosemary Bigby, Councilmember Florence A. Jackson

City of Arcola Mayors

Mike R. Saenz	1981—1993
Linda Deleon	May 1994- May 1996
Abraham Jones	May 1996—September 1996
Alvin Gipson	September 1996—May 2000
Lee Roy Jackson	May 2000—May 2004
Alvin Gipson	May 2004—May 2006
Tom Tuffly	May 2006—May 2008
Mary Etta Anderson	May 2008—May 2012
Evelyn Jones	May 2012—May 2014
Mary Etta Anderson	May 2014—May 2018
Fred A. Burton	May 2018—May 2024
Dr. Veeda Williams	May 2024—

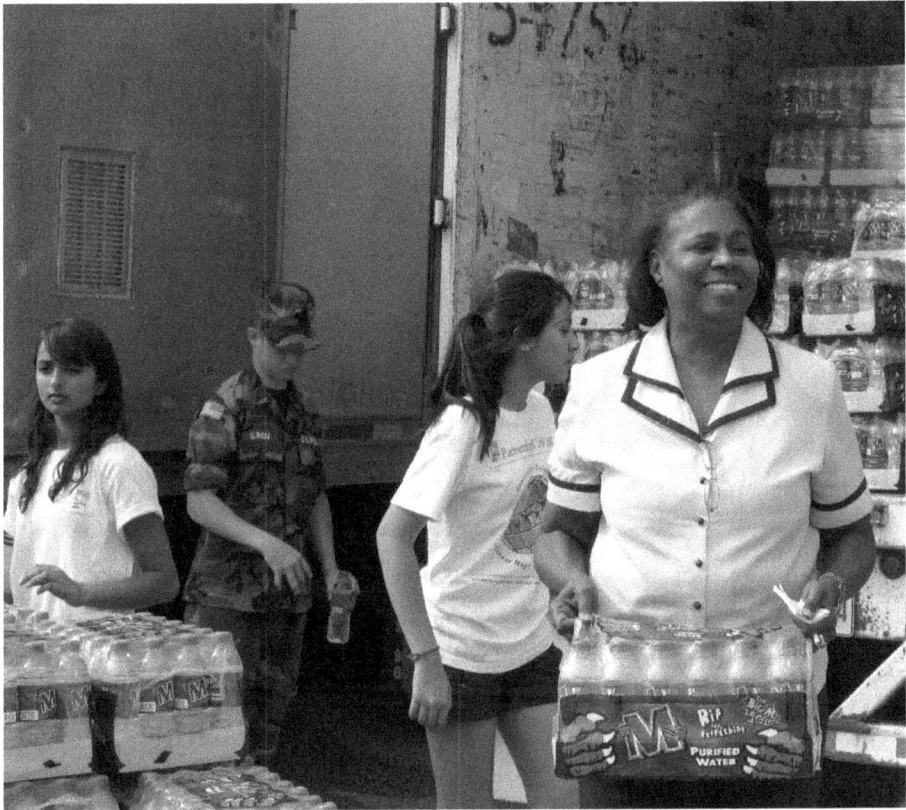

Mary Etta Anderson

Mary Etta Anderson was elected the city's first Black American female mayor, beginning her first term in May 2008 and winning re-election in May 2010, marking a significant transformation period for the city. *We are facing some critical issues in Arcola: Water, sewage, cleaning up our city, and developing sound educational programs for our youth, senior citizens, and citizens in general.* She prioritized upgrades to the city's water, streets, and drainage systems, ensuring better living conditions for citizens and on April 18, 2012, the USDA awarded a $3,440,000 loan and grant to the City of Arcola for its water system. Her leadership was crucial following Hurricane Ike, as she spearheaded recovery efforts to help the community rebuild.

In addition to enhancing the infrastructure, Anderson implemented code enforcement measures to maintain and improve the city's

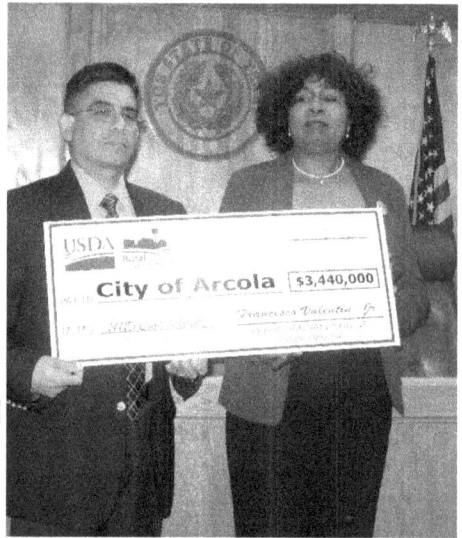

standards and appearance. She upgraded the trash pickup system, including introducing heavy trash pickup. Anderson's commitment to the community extended to revitalizing homes for low-income seniors in collaboration with Fort Bend Corp officials, providing much needed support for vulnerable residents.

One of Anderson's notable achievements was the design and construction of the Arcola Community Center, which became a hub for community activities and events. She also launched a community computer lab that offered residents, including seniors, training in various software and free Internet access. Her forward-thinking approach led her to explore using rainwater harvesting for the city's municipal water system, promoting sustainable water management.

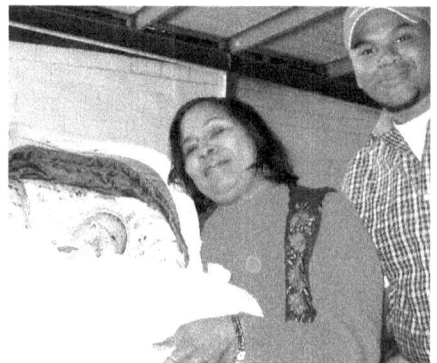

During her third and fourth terms, 2014-2018, Anderson focused on improving the city's infrastructure and services. Under her leadership, the city constructed a new sewer treatment plant and improved sanitation and infrastructure. Anderson's dedication to enhancing Arcola and her efforts to improve the community's services left a lasting impact. Her vision helped shape a better future for Arcola's residents, setting a standard for future leaders to follow.

Arika Carr

On September 19, 2022, Arika Carr was appointed as Arcola's first female Chief of Police, making her the first African American woman to hold this position in Fort Bend County. The city council unanimously approved her appointment after a period of controversy and leadership changes within the Arcola Police Department.

Carr began her law enforcement career in 2010 and joined the Arcola Police Department in 2017. Her dedication to the community and proactive approach to community policing have been significant assets to the department. As Chief of Police, Carr aims to rebuild trust within the community and enhance the department's reputation. She plans to promote transparency, increase community engagement, and conduct monthly officer training.

Carr envisions making the Arcola Police Department one of the best in Texas while ensuring a safe and crime-free environment for the community. Her leadership is viewed as a positive step toward achieving these goals.

Modern Day Arcola

On May 4, 2024, Dr. Veeda V. Williams was elected Mayor of the great City of Arcola. A proud native with deep roots in the community, Dr. Williams brings a fresh perspective and bold vision for Arcola's future. Her leadership is guided by a profound understanding of local needs, and she is dedicated to fostering a united and thriving city for all. Committed to amplifying the voices of Arcola's residents, Dr. Williams aims to deliver practical solutions to the challenges the city faces.

Under her leadership, Arcola embodies resilience and determination. Though small, the city remains steadfast in its commitment to economic development and enhancing the quality of life. Together, the community and its leaders continue to pave the way for a brighter, more promising future for all its residents.

Arcola's Demographics

Over the course of 225 years, Arcola has transitioned from a sparsely populated prairie used by Indigenous peoples to a plantation-based society and, eventually, to a diverse, rapidly growing suburb at the edge of Houston's sprawl. Before 1822, the land was part of vast prairies in southeastern Texas, used seasonally by the Karankawa, Tonkawa, and possibly the Akokisa peoples for hunting, gathering, and temporary camps. European American settlement began after Mexico granted land to members of the Old Three Hundred colonists, including the David Fitzgerald League, which became Arcola's foundation. *While the David Fitzgerald League marks the legal origin of land ownership in the area, Arcola's civic and educational foundation was laid by freed Black families in Abstracts 25, 31, 170, and 352. These abstracts represent the true beginning of Arcola as a living, self-determined settlement.*

By the mid-19th century, large cotton and sugar plantations dominated the area. Jonathan Dawson Waters acquired the entire Fitzgerald League by 1850, creating one of the region's largest plantations. The enslaved population—often outnumbering free Whites-reflected Fort Bend County's status as one of the Texas counties with a majority Black population in this era. Estimates suggest several dozen free Whites and several hundred enslaved Blacks lived on plantations across what would later be incorporated as Arcola.

The end of slavery in 1865 brought profound changes. Freedmen formed the nucleus of Arcola's earliest permanent Black community, building churches, schools, and cemeteries that remain key to the city's historical identity. Economic depression and natural disasters slowed growth, but these institutions anchored the community for generations.

Throughout the late 19th and early 20th centuries, Arcola's population remained small and rural, growing modestly until suburban expansion began after World War II. Improved transportation and Houston's outward growth attracted new residents, setting the stage for the rapid changes that have occurred since 1990, when Latino families began arriving in large numbers, shifting the city from a historically Black majority to today's Latino majority. Arcola remains youthful, with a median age around 29, a high share of households with children, and a demographic profile that mirrors wider Texas trends.

Arcola, Texas — Population by Major Census Year (1850–2025)

Year	Estimated Population	Notes/Source
1850	~300–500	Plantation records, inferred from county data
1860	~400–600	Plantation labor expansion
1870	~300–400	Post-emancipation decline
1880	~350–400	Railroad arrival boosts modest recovery
1890	~50–100*	1890 Census mostly lost
1900	~50	Two schools, a small settlement
1910	~50	Rural outpost
1920	~60	Stable population
1930	~80	Slight growth
1940	~100	Pre-WWII growth signs
1950	~120	Post-war uptick
1960	~150	Early suburbanization
1970	~200–300	Houston's proximity draws settlers
1980	~300–666	Pre-incorporation counts vary
1990	666	Official Census
2000	1,048–1,053	Accelerated influx
2010	1,640–1,642	Rapid growth
2020	2,034–2,057	Latino majority emerges
2021	2,156	Peak before pandemic fluctuation
2023	2,050	COVID-19 impact
2025	2,346 (est.)	Projected rebound

*Earlier years are estimates from regional/county sources.

Historical Demographic Narrative

1850–1940: Plantation Economy, Emancipation, and Rural Stability

The 1850 census for Fort Bend County recorded a majority Black population, dominated by enslaved labor. By 1860, plantation culture was at its peak; the 1858 arrival of the Houston Tap Railroad began connecting the area to wider markets. Emancipation brought land and livelihood changes, with many Freedmen remaining as tenant farmers while others migrated.

Rail expansion in 1878 (Gulf, Colorado & Santa Fe Railroad) made Arcola a regional junction, yet population growth remained slow. In 1903, schools served 42 White and 176 Black pupils, underscoring entrenched segregation. Through 1940, the population held near 100–120, supported by local institutions despite economic hardship.

1950–1990: Suburban Links and Incorporation

Postwar transport links and Houston's growth spurred gradual population increases, from 150 in 1960 to roughly 300–400 by 1980. Incorporation in 1981 gave the city governance over its development. By 1990, the population officially reached 666, with growing racial and ethnic diversity.

1990–2025: Metroplex Expansion and Demographic Shifts
Population Growth

Arcola's population has more than tripled since 1990, climbing from 666 to a projected 2,346 in 2025. Between 2000 and 2023 alone, growth exceeded 122%, driven by suburban migration, affordable housing, and proximity to Houston employment centers.

Racial/Ethnic Change

The city's demographic center shifted decisively toward a Latino majority status after 2010:

Year	Hispanic/ Latino	White (NH)	Black (NH)	Asian	Native Amer.	Multiracial	Other
2010	51.9%	34.3%	34.2%	2.2%	0.4%	1.9%	27.1%
2020	66.8%	7.6%	22.5%	1.2%	0.05%	1.7%	1.2%
2023	76.1%	7.5%*	16.4%	<2%	<1%	~4%	NA

*White and Hispanic categories overlap in ACS data.
Black residents remain culturally and institutionally significant, even as their share of the population has decreased.

Age Structure

Arcola remains younger than Texas (median ~35.5) and the U.S. (~38):
- 2010: Median Age 28
- 2021: Median Age 26.6
- 2023: Median Age 29.7

Youth under 18 make up nearly 38% of the population, reflecting high birth rates and family-oriented households.

Income and Inequality

Median household income rose from $60,380 in 2010 to $73,778 in 2023, with fluctuations due to economic cycles. The Gini coefficient (0.3729) shows moderate inequality; the top 5% of households earn over $300,000, while the bottom quintile averages $24,230.

Education

High school completion reached 79.3% in 2021, but bachelor's degree attainment lags at ~10%, far below state and county levels. Barriers include a high share of recent immigrants and economic constraints.

Migration

Since 1990, growth has been fueled by:

- Latino migration from Mexico and Central America
- Domestic in-migration from the Houston metro
- Smaller Asian and other immigrant groups since the 2000s

By 2023, 21.1% of residents were foreign-born, 99% from Latin America.

Housing and Household Composition

Housing units expanded from under 200 in 1990 to 788 in 2021. Nearly 35% were built since 2000. Median home value in 2023 was $182,700, with a 66% homeownership rate. Households average 3.1–3.6 persons; family households average 4.06, with many multigenerational arrangements.

Conclusion: Patterns, Challenges, and Outlook

Arcola's demographic evolution from 1800 to 2025 reflects resilience and transformation, from Indigenous stewardship to plantations, post-emancipation Black community building, and 21st-century suburban growth. Challenges persist in educational attainment, income inequality, and economic diversification. Rapid growth strains infrastructure, yet the city's youthful, diverse population offers a foundation for inclusive development.

Future success will depend on strategic investment in education, infrastructure, and local institutions that honor Arcola's layered history. As part of the greater Houston narrative, Arcola exemplifies the blending of histories, cultures, and aspirations that will continue to shape Texas's social landscape for generations.

From Brush Arbors to Blue Ridge

The Arc of Black Education in Arcola

In the wake of Emancipation, Arcola's earliest classrooms sprang to
life beneath brush arbors, where local elders and ministers taught
reading and arithmetic under open skies. U.S. Census records from
1870 show 18 Black and 4 White school-age children living in Arcola
households. By the 1880s, Sunday schools at St. Paul CME and St.
John Missionary Baptist added informal weekday instruction,
sustaining communal learning until the fledgling Arcola Independent
School District took shape in the late 1890s.

Among the earliest known educators in Arcola, Reverend J.H. Bell
served as both teacher and trustee affiliated with St. Paul CME

Church. His name appears in Freedmen's Bureau rolls and early school census records, where he is listed as an instructor from the late 1870s through 1915. Bell's dual role as spiritual leader and educator helped formalize weekday instruction on church grounds, laying the foundation for Arcola's first permanent Black school sites.

According to Art Eilers' account, when his family moved to Arcola in 1903, the first school he attended was a makeshift classroom set up in a sheep shed. Later, he attended a school referred to as Rural District No. 15, Fort Bend (Bones, Frances, 1968). County superintendent filings from 1900 indicate that 94 Black pupils were enrolled in Arcola schools. Official records from 1903 list four Black campuses serving 176 students, including the newly recorded Arcola Colored School beside St. John Missionary Baptist. Around 1905, parents and church members replaced borrowed church space with a dedicated one-room frame building. Mrs. Sarah Jane Taylor taught in the one-room frame school that replaced borrowed church space in 1905. Affiliated with Mount Zion Baptist Church, she served as both educator and church matron, maintaining civic continuity across generations. Her teaching career spanned from the 1880s through 1950, and she is remembered in oral histories as a disciplinarian, caretaker, and curriculum steward during Arcola's formative years.

As enrollment swelled, its pupils moved in 1910 from the one-room frame school to a purpose-built successor, Mustang School. The Mustang School, established in Abstract 170 just east of Arcola's sugar-mill fields, marked the district's full embrace of public education for grades one through four. Hired year by year, itinerant teachers delivered lessons in a simple one-room frame structure. By 1910, Mustang School had recorded 106 Black pupils. Mrs. Lucinda Hayes, affiliated with St. Paul CME Church, served as both educator and church matron from 1910 through 1955. She taught across multiple sites in Abstract 170, including the pre-Rosenwald parcel and later Oaklane School. Hayes appears in school census records and oral history interviews, remembered for her quiet discipline and unwavering commitment to Black children's education.

Mustang School Bell

Mrs. Myra Ann Evans shared vivid memories of the one-room schoolhouse, Mustang School, which accommodated students from 1st through 8th grade. *Boys and girls sat on opposite sides of the room, and students used secondhand books passed down from white schools, as they were never provided with new materials. Miss Norman rang the school bell every day, though it was broken and held together with a piece of wire she had fastened.*

During Mrs. Myra Ann's time at the Mustang School, a three-room school, Oaklane School, was built on the same property. By 1915, Oaklane School had expanded to serve 122 students. It was formally listed under Arcola ISD in 1920 with 138 Black pupils enrolled. Enrollment rose to 144 by 1925 and 156 by 1930, according to TEA biennial reports and county superintendent records.

Mrs. Myra Ann believes the old school Mustang building was eventually donated to the Masonic Lodge. The teaching staff included Miss Summerfield, who taught grades 1 through 3, and Miss Dora Norman, who managed grades 4 through 6. Coach Curtis Solomon oversaw physical education and encouraged students to participate in activities like basketball. An outside instructor from the city occasionally visited to provide lessons for the Glee Club, which Mrs. Myra Ann fondly recalled joining. She also participated in basketball under Coach Solomon's guidance. Mrs. Otavia Carrie Thorton Williams served as both the teacher for 7th and 8th grades and the principal, playing a central role in the school's daily operations.

According to Mrs. Willie Jean Hayes, about 50 students from Arcola, Fresno, and Hawdon attended school in Arcola. They would ride the school bus to Houston to attend Jack Yates High School if they wanted to continue their high school education. Mr. Lester Louis was the school bus driver. Hayes attended Yates for two years before being transferred to M.R. Wood School in Sugar Land.

Oaklane School, under the Arcola Independent School District, became a vibrant hub of learning, where homegrown educators led music recitals, civic meetings, and the beloved *Oaklane Panthers* softball and baseball teams gave youth a sense of competitive pride. Church fundraisers underwrote equipment, and Friday night games drew crowds from across the district, reinforcing bonds that school walls alone could never contain.

A 1907 land deed confirms that a parcel within Abstract 31 was donated by the Mount Zion community for *religious and educational purposes*. A 1912 ledger entry from Mount Zion Missionary Baptist

Church references *schooling of the children* held on the grounds. Cross-referenced with the 1910 census listing Reverend J.H. Bell and his school-age children, this confirms that informal instruction occurred on the Abstract 31 parcel prior to Oaklane's construction. Bell also served as a trustee for Arcola Colored School, anchoring early civic and instructional leadership.

Residential census data from 1930 shows approximately 61 Black and 25 white school-age children living in Arcola. While Black students attended Mustang and Oaklane, White students were increasingly bused to Missouri City Elementary and Sugar Land Junior High. Zoning overlays from 1930 to 1969 show that white students in Arcola were assigned to Missouri City Elementary, Sugar Land Junior High, and later Dulles High School. Bus routes operated along FM 521, McKeever Road, and Trammel-Fresno Road. No white-only schools operated within Arcola after 1903, though white families remained present in the area.

Although governed locally by Arcola ISD, county records often grouped its schools under Missouri City ISD for administrative convenience. As a rural common school district, Arcola lacked its own superintendent infrastructure and tax office. Fort Bend County grouped it with larger districts like Missouri City ISD to centralize transportation routes, payroll processing, teacher assignments, and reporting structures across multiple segregated schools. This arrangement streamlined operations but did not reflect jurisdictional control or educational autonomy. Arcola's schools remained locally led, with deep ties to community churches, civic organizations, and parent advocates.

The Rosenwald School in Arcola was part of a transformative initiative launched in the early 20th century to improve educational access for

Black children in the rural South. Funded through a partnership between Booker T. Washington and philanthropist Julius Rosenwald, the program required matching contributions from local Black communities, often in the form of land, labor, and materials. In Arcola, Reverend Elijah Carter donated land in 1928 (Abstract 352), enabling the construction of a two-teacher rural school that followed Rosenwald's standardized architectural plans emphasizing natural light, ventilation, and functional design. Though listed under Missouri City ISD for administrative purposes, the Rosenwald School was conceived, built, and sustained by Arcola families. Miss Louisa M. Carter taught at the Rosenwald School and later at Oaklane Elementary, serving from 1925 through 1961. A lifelong educator affiliated with St. Paul CME Church, Carter appears in TEA census filings and Rosenwald rosters. Her tenure bridged the Rosenwald era and Fort Bend ISD consolidation, and she is remembered for her rigor, warmth, and commitment to civic uplift through education.

Mr. Isaiah Green served as a teacher at the Rosenwald School from 1915 through 1945. A deacon at St. Paul CME Church, Green's name appears in county superintendent reports and oral testimony. His instruction emphasized literacy, civic responsibility, and agricultural education. Green's death around 1945 marked the end of a long and respected teaching career rooted in community service.

Earlier filings misattributed the Rosenwald School to Abstract 352. However, its physical location at the corner of McKeever Road and FM 521 confirms its placement within Abstract 170. It stood as a symbol of community resilience and self-determination, serving generations of Black students with dignity despite the constraints of segregation. Enrollment at Rosenwald began with 88 Black pupils in 1928, rising to 102 by 1935, 118 by 1945, and peaking at 261 in 1969, its final year of operation.

In April 1959, the people of Arcola made a pivotal decision: by public vote, they approved the consolidation of the Arcola Independent School District with Fort Bend ISD. This was not a passive shift, it was a deliberate choice by local families and leaders to seek broader educational opportunities, including expanded curricula, vocational training, and upgraded facilities. While Fort Bend ISD absorbed Arcola's campuses, community advocates negotiated to preserve long-standing traditions, retain veteran teachers, and secure representation on the newly unified school board. The vote marked both a closing chapter and a bold new beginning for Black education in Arcola.

This decision marked the end of Arcola Independent District's status and brought schools like Oaklane Elementary under Fort Bend ISD governance. Though often overlooked in district histories, Arcola's participation was pivotal, reflecting the civic agency of its Black community and shaping the educational trajectory of Fort Bend County during the final decade of segregation. At the time of consolidation, Oaklane Elementary (Abstract 170) served 163 Black pupils. Rosenwald School (Abstract 170) continued under Fort Bend ISD with 172 enrolled.

Under this new structure, the original Oaklane School was reclassified as Oaklane Elementary, becoming Arcola's sole campus for Black children in grades one through eight. Older students were redirected to M.R. Wood School in Sugar Land. Though the building remained physically unchanged, Oaklane Elementary operated under a different philosophy, one shaped by Fort Bend Independent School District mandates and the slow, uneven progression toward desegregation. The school's independence faded, and its role shifted from a community-built institution to a segregation-era holding school, designed to meet state requirements while maintaining racial separation.

By September 1965, as desegregation policies took effect, Oaklane Elementary closed its doors. Students were seamlessly relocated to Annie Wilcox Elementary, housed in the former Missouri City High School building. District planners coordinated bus routes, PTA welcome breakfasts, and joint assemblies to ensure familiar faces, extracurricular clubs, and community ties accompanied every pupil. The hand-off demonstrated how thoughtful planning could transform a seismic shift into a shared milestone.

Even in closure, Oaklane Elementary left behind a legacy of resilience, adaptation, and quiet resistance. Its students and teachers became part of the broader narrative of educational integration in Fort Bend County, helping to shape a more inclusive public school system. The memory of Oaklane endures, not just as a building, but as a chapter in the long struggle for dignity, equity, and belonging.

Four years later, the brand-new Blue Ridge Elementary rose on state-of-the-art grounds, welcoming former Arcola students into a fully integrated campus. Bright classrooms replaced reclaimed hallways, yet many of Oaklane's teachers, coaches, and community-led traditions guided the transition. As children filed through the doors, they carried forward a legacy woven through Smoke-filled brush arbors, church pews, and storied schoolhouses, a testament to Arcola's enduring faith in education.

Following the consolidation, the district set its sights on growth and development. Fort Bend Independent School District purchased a site on Dulles Avenue (formerly known as Lester Road), and construction began on the Administration Building and John Foster Dulles High School. The Administration Building was ready for use by the summer of 1961. This marked a significant step in the growth and evolution of Fort Bend ISD. Fort Bend ISD proudly celebrated its first graduating class in 1960, and the inaugural class from the current

Dulles High School graduated in 1962. After desegregation, Dulles High was the only zoned high school in the district until Willowridge High School in Houston opened in 1979. That same year, Oaklane Elementary building was sold to Fort Bend County. The first integrated class to graduate from Dulles High School was in 1966. Monroe Williams was a member of this notable class, as it was the first to graduate from the school after its establishment.

Over the years, the zoning of Fort Bend Independent School District schools has undergone several changes. Before the opening of Hightower in 1998, Elkins High School served Arcola. After 1998 and before 2010, all Arcola pupils were zoned to Hightower. Before 2018, most of Arcola was zoned to Baines Middle School. Rapid residential growth in the FM 521 corridor and surrounding subdivisions began to strain Baines' capacity, prompting Fort Bend ISD to review attendance boundaries. District planners proposed a rezoning to balance enrollment, reduce overcrowding, and shorten bus routes for students living south of Highway 6 and east of FM 521. In 2018, a significant portion of Arcola was rezoned to Thornton Middle School. Before 2023, portions of Arcola south of Highway 6 were zoned to Ridge Point High School; that year, they were rezoned to Crawford.

In 2026, the Fort Bend Independent School District (FBISD) will open Middle School 16 in Arcola, Texas. This significant investment marks the first time FBISD has allocated over $100 million to a single project in Arcola. The new middle school is situated on the FM 521 Corridor.

On December 17, 2018, the Fort Bend ISD Board approved Corgan, a nationally recognized architecture and design firm, to develop the construction documents and specifications for Middle School 16. The school's design incorporates cutting-edge sustainability features, positioning it to become the district's first Net-Zero campus, capable of producing as much energy as it consumes. According to the 2023 Bond, $82 million was initially budgeted for the project, but the final allocation reached $106.5 million. Construction began in fall 2024, with completion anticipated by August 2026, in time for the 2026–2027 academic year.

The Naming Committee for Middle School 16 was established by Fort Bend ISD as per Board Policy CW (Local). The FBISD community was invited to nominate names via an electronic form from March 21 to April 2, 2025. Nearly 1,200 submissions were received. District staff reviewed the submissions, compiled duplicates, and removed names already used in the district (e.g., Anne Sullivan, Barbara Jordan). Each nomination included a summary of biographical or historical data justifying the name.

The Middle School 16 Naming Committee met on May 15, 2025. The Department of Collaborative Communities led the school naming process, with committee members including Board of Trustees representatives Sonya Jones and Shirley Rose-Gilliam, principals, parents, teachers, students, and community representatives from neighboring schools.

The Naming Committee selected Amy Coleman as the proposed namesake for Middle School 16. Amy Joyce Davis Coleman was a dedicated educator and humanitarian who made significant contributions to the field of education over her nearly 33-year career. She was the first in her family to earn both a bachelor's and a master's degree, showcasing her commitment to academic excellence. Coleman received several lifetime achievement awards in education, including the MKO Alpha Kappa Alpha Educational Excellence Award.

Her involvement extended beyond the classroom. She was actively engaged with the NAACP Missouri City chapter, Friends of the Missouri City Library, and the National Society for Black Educators (NASBE). Additionally, she was a founding board member of the Southwest Educational Project (SWEP), a local non-profit that organized tours of historically Black colleges and universities across the country for over a decade.

Coleman's legacy is marked by her dedication to improving educational opportunities and her active participation in community

organizations. Her selection as the namesake for Middle School 16 is a fitting tribute to her lifelong commitment to education and community service.

Middle School 16's opening represents not only a major infrastructural milestone but also a symbolic continuation of Arcola's long tradition of community-driven education, stretching from brush arbor gatherings in the 19th century, through the era of Rosenwald and Oaklane, to a 21st-century campus designed to meet the needs of a diverse and growing population.

As of 2025, students residing in Arcola are served by a network of Fort Bend ISD schools organized into distinct zoning tiers. The Primary Zone, which encompasses most of Arcola proper, includes *Heritage Rose Elementary School* for grades PK–5, *Billy Baines Middle School* for grades 6–8, and *Ridge Point High School* for grades 9–12. Families living in the Secondary Zone, which covers areas north and east of State Highway 6 and north and west of FM 521, are zoned to *Burton Elementary School*, *Lake Olympia Middle School*, and *Hightower High*

School. Additionally, several campuses fall within Boundary-Adjacent and New Development Zones, which may apply to fringe subdivisions or be subject to future rezoning. These include *Donald Leonetti Elementary School*, *Alyssa Ferguson Elementary School*, *Ronald Thornton Middle School*, and *Almeta Crawford High School*. This tiered structure reflects both current enrollment patterns and anticipated growth across Arcola's expanding residential footprint.

The history of education in Arcola is marked by significant milestones and the unwavering dedication of key educators. From the early establishment of schools to the impactful reforms led by figures like Reverend J.H. Bell, Mrs. Sarah Jane Taylor, and Mrs. Lucinda Hayes, each event has contributed to shaping the educational landscape of the community. The legacy of these educational pioneers continues to influence the present, fostering a culture of learning and growth. As we look to the future, it is essential to build on this rich heritage, ensuring that the values of education and community development remain at the forefront of our efforts. The ongoing initiatives and future plans will undoubtedly carry forward the spirit of progress and innovation, securing a brighter future for the generations to come.

Arcola's Educational Milestones

Year	Local Milestone	Broader Context
1870s	First brush-arbor classes on plantation grounds	Reconstruction era brings new hopes and limits
1872	Arcola Colored School opens in Abstract 170 with 38 Black pupils	Freedmen's Bureau confirms early Black education
1880s	Informal weekday/Sunday schools at St. Paul CME & St. John Baptist	Jim Crow laws hardened segregation in Texas
Late 1890s	Arcola Independent School District takes shape	Populist movement peaks in rural America
1903	State report lists 6 AISD campuses (4 Black, 2 White)	Plessy v. Ferguson (1896) governs *separate but equal*
1905	Community builds first dedicated Arcola Colored School frame building (Abstract 170)	Wright brothers' flight sparks new possibilities
1907	Mount Zion community donates land in Abstract 31 for *religious and educational purposes*	Black churches expand civic and educational roles
1910	Pupils shift to Mustang School (Abstract 170), first formal public facility	NAACP founded (1909), push for Black rights begins
1920	Oaklane School formally listed under Arcola ISD with 138 Black pupils	Rural education reforms gain traction
1928	Reverend Elijah Carter donates land for Rosenwald School (Abstract 170)	Rosenwald Fund expands Black rural schooling

Year	Local Milestone	Broader Context
1930s	Oaklane Panthers baseball/softball teams emerge; music recitals flourish	Great Depression strains small-town budgets
1940	Oaklane becomes Arcola's primary Black campus; Mustang phased out	WWII reshapes labor and education priorities
1954	Brown v. Board of Education decision	Legal mandate to desegregate public schools
April 1959	Voters approve AISD's consolidation into Fort Bend ISD	Sputnik prompts U.S. investment in education
1965	Oaklane Elementary closes; students reassigned to Annie Wilcox Elementary	Civil Rights Act (1964) accelerates integration
1969	Rosenwald School closes; Blue Ridge Elementary opens as integrated campus	Apollo 11 moon landing symbolizes new frontiers
1970s	Arcola students zoned to Dulles High School	Desegregation reshapes district boundaries
1998	Hightower High School opens; Arcola students rezoned	FBISD expands to meet suburban growth
2018	Thornton Middle School opens; Arcola zoning shifts again	Equity in middle school access becomes priority
2023	Arcola students south of Hwy 6 rezoned to Crawford High School	District responds to demographic shifts
2026	Middle School 16 opens on FM 521 Corridor (Abstract 170)	FBISD's first Net-Zero campus and $100M investment

Octavia Carrie Thornton Williams

Octavia Carrie Thornton Williams was born on October 19, 1913, in Richmond, Texas, and died on April 9, 1992. She was the daughter of George Thornton and Harriett Julia Jones Thornton, respected operators of a colored restaurant on Railroad Street in Richmond, a corridor central to Black enterprise and community life in Fort Bend County. Census records from 1920 and 1930 confirm her upbringing in their household alongside her siblings: Nettie, Rosalie, and Lawyer.

Williams began her teaching career in 1934 at the Arcola Plantation (House Plantation), where she served rural Black children until 1947. That year, she was appointed principal and teacher at Arcola Elementary Colored School, part of the Missouri City Colored School District. At the time, the school operated out of a frame building with practically no modern conveniences, serving 105–110 students with four teachers and one of the district's two buses.

Arcola's schools were listed under Missouri City ISD in certain records due to county-level administrative grouping, not formal district governance. As a rural common school district, Arcola lacked its own superintendent and tax office infrastructure. Fort Bend County grouped it with larger districts like Missouri City ISD for logistical oversight, a bureaucratic strategy to centralize transportation routes, payroll processing, teacher assignments, and reporting structures across multiple segregated schools. This arrangement streamlined operations but did not reflect jurisdictional control or educational autonomy.

Williams taught grades 6, 7, and 8, while Mary Summerfield led the primary department, Freddie Lee Jackson taught grades 3, 4, and 5, and Curtis Solomon directed athletics at both Arcola and Missouri City Elementary Colored Schools.

Believing that the children of Arcola deserved better, Williams led the transformation of the school's facilities. Under her leadership, a new modern four-classroom building was constructed, recognized as one of the most outstanding schools serving Black children in Fort Bend County. Her guiding philosophy was captured in her own words: *Standing for God and humanity first, last, and at all time.*

She earned her undergraduate credentials from Prairie View State Normal & Industrial College in 1939 and completed her master's degree at Texas Southern University, appearing in the 1949 Texas Southern University yearbook under the Education section.
Her appointment was publicly confirmed in a contemporaneous newspaper article titled *Principal Octavia (Berkley) Williams, Another Highly Educated Young Colored Woman Presides As Principal Over Arcola Elementary Colored School, Fort Bend County.* The article praised her as a brilliant teacher and administrator. Her leadership remains a benchmark in the history of Black education in Fort Bend Church bulletins from Antioch Missionary Baptist Church and Mt. Carmel Missionary Baptist Church in Houston reference her contributions as an educator and speaker.

Billy Jefferson BJ Baines

Billy Jefferson Baines was born on May 16, 1928, in Wharton, Texas, the youngest of seven children raised by Tressie and Callie Baines. A devoted husband to Joyce Lee Hilliard and father to John, Ronald, Billy, and Michelle. BJ Baines built a life defined by integrity, mentorship, and civic leadership.

Before entering education, Baines served in the United States Army from 1950 to 1952, during the Korean War. He attained the rank of Corporal, and his military service shaped the discipline, resilience, and leadership he carried into every classroom and campus. He was later buried with honors at Houston National Cemetery, a final tribute to his service and sacrifice.

After returning from military duty, Baines earned his bachelor's degree in education from Prairie View A&M University in 1955, followed by graduate studies at Texas Southern University, which he completed in the early 1960s. These institutions, both historically Black universities, equipped him with the academic foundation and civic vision that would define his career.

In 1956, Baines began teaching social studies in the Sugar Land Independent School District, three years before the formation of Fort Bend ISD. At the time, the region's schools were racially segregated and operated under separate jurisdictions: Sugar Land Elementary served white students, while M.R. Wood School served Black students. Nearby, Arcola maintained its own independent school district, with separate governance and facilities. Baines's early tenure placed him at the heart of a segregated system on the brink of transformation.

In 1959, following the merger of Sugar Land ISD, Missouri City ISD, and Arcola ISD into the newly formed Fort Bend Independent School District (FBISD), Superintendent L.P. Rodgers appointed Baines as principal of Arcola Elementary. This made him the first Black principal in Fort Bend ISD, a historic breakthrough in educational equity and representation. *He was the first Black principal I ever saw,* recalled a former student. *That mattered. It told me I could lead too.*

Baines later served as principal at Blue Ridge Elementary, where he recruited a pioneering team of Black educators, including Amy Coleman, who began as a first-grade teacher in 1970 and later became principal of Briargate Elementary. *He recruited me when I was fresh out of college,* Coleman remembered. *Told me, We're building something bigger than a school, we're building legacy. I never forgot that.*

While Baines is the first principal confirmed by named record at Blue Ridge, current documentation does not confirm him as the founding principal. His leadership during the school's formative years remains widely recognized and deeply impactful.

In January 1979, Baines was appointed founding principal of Lantern Lane Elementary, where he led the opening of a new campus with vision, care, and community-centered leadership. *Mr. Baines was more than a principal; he was a mentor, a father figure, and a pillar of our community,* said a retired educator. *He saw potential in every child and made sure we saw it too.* He also served at Oak Lane Junior High, where his steady hand and deep commitment to educational excellence shaped generations of students and staff.

In 2006, Fort Bend ISD honored his legacy by naming its 12th middle school in Sienna Plantation the Billy J. Baines Middle School. Unlike many honorees, Baines lived to witness this tribute, attending the dedication of a campus that continues to serve thousands of students in his name. *Billy Baines was the kind of leader who didn't just open doors, he held them open for the next generation,* said a board member at the ceremony.

He passed away on October 24, 2010, at age 82. His memorial service was held at Trinity United Methodist Church in Houston, and he was laid to rest at Houston National Cemetery. His legacy endures in the lives of the students he mentored, the educators he empowered, and the civic record he helped shape.

March 13, 1994

2939 Payson St.
Houston, Texas 77021

To Whom It May Concern:

I am pleased to write this positive letter of recommendation for Veeda Williams. I was honored to serve as her Elementary School Principal. Veeda was an excellent, honor roll student, mannerable, bright and always co-operative. During her last year in the elementary school, she was selected by her peers as the OUTSTANDING Young Lady for that year. Veeda will be an asset to any organization.

Respectfully,

Billy J. Baines

Retired Principal
Fort Bend Independent School District

Amy Joyce Davis Coleman

Amy Joyce Davis Coleman was a visionary educator whose 33-year career reshaped the civic and academic landscape of Fort Bend County, Texas. From her first-grade classroom at Blue Ridge Elementary to her founding principalship at Hunters Glen, Coleman built not just schools, but systems of care, leadership, and generational impact. Her legacy lives in the students she inspired, the educators she mentored, and the civic institutions she helped shape.

Coleman began teaching in 1970 at Blue Ridge Elementary, where she served as Mistress of Ceremonies for the school's Black History Program, anchoring cultural pride in a region where such recognition was rare. Her classroom was a haven of rigor, affirmation, and emotional warmth. Krista Coleman,

136

Amy's daughter, shared that *she gave me a set of encyclopedias for my ninth birthday,* a reflection of her mother's belief in knowledge as empowerment and her lifelong commitment to learning.

By 1979, she was serving as assistant principal at Briargate Elementary School, mentoring staff, guiding curriculum, and building deep relationships with families. A photograph from that year shows her attending a Thanksgiving event at the school with her second-grade daughter, a moment that anchors her administrative timeline and community visibility.

In 1981, Coleman succeeded as principal, becoming the first Black woman to lead a campus in the Fort Bend Independent School District. Her leadership was strategic and deeply rooted in community trust. She built systems of accountability, cultivated talent, and anchored Briargate as a civic institution. Then in 1985, Coleman made history again as the founding principal of Hunters Glen Elementary, where she

handpicked her staff and shaped the school's identity from the ground up.

Sheila Mutton Hutchings stated, *she recruited me from Michigan to teach in Fort Bend. It changed my life.* Coleman's reach extended far beyond her own campuses; she traveled across state lines to recruit educators, mentor new leaders, and build a pipeline of excellence that shaped the district for decades.

Her educational philosophy was grounded in rigorous scholarship, spiritual faith, and service. Family testimony affirms that she *loved God, had a huge faith,* and believed deeply in perseverance and civic duty. According to Darla Fagan, a longtime FBISD colleague, *she could always see the silver lining in every cloud. She was known for her perfect posture, radiant smile, and ability to remember every name, comfort every fear, and inspire every child.*

Wendi Johnson-Turner, a former student, recalled that *Mrs. Coleman taught me how to read... She is one of the reasons I am a teacher today.* Her influence was generational, shaping not just students but future educators and civic leaders.

Coleman served with distinction on boards including the NAACP, Friends of the Missouri City Library, and the Southwest Educational Project, which conducted HBCU tours for over a decade. She was honored with the Alpha Kappa Alpha Educational Excellence Award, and her civic footprint extended across Fort Bend County. As Marvin King, a Missouri City community member, reflected, *Mrs. Coleman was a fixture in the Missouri City community. She made a definitive impact in my life and the lives of many others by upholding the standards of excellence and demonstrating the spirit of love.*

Amy Coleman passed away in 2005, leaving behind a legacy of excellence, mentorship, and community stewardship. Nearly two decades later, in May 2025, Fort Bend ISD named its 16th middle school in her honor, a posthumous recognition of her enduring influence and the community's deep respect for her achievements and values. The naming committee received 11,197 submissions, and her selection reflects not just institutional memory but generational gratitude.

At the school's Topping Out Ceremony on June 25, 2025, Dr. Krista Coleman declared, *We aren't just marking the completion of a building; we are laying the foundation for possibility, purpose, and the brilliance waiting to rise.*

Amy Coleman's name belongs not just in district records but in the civic memory of Fort Bend County. She was not just a principal; she was an architect of possibility.

Emergency Management

Policing and firefighting are two of the most essential services a municipality provides. As the city's service area expands through voluntary annexation, maintaining quick response times is becoming increasingly crucial.

The Arcola Police Department

Before establishing the Arcola Police Department, the Fort Bend County Sheriff's Office provided law enforcement services in the area. The Sheriff's Office was responsible for maintaining law and order, responding to emergencies, and offering general law enforcement services to the residents of Arcola.

The Arcola Police Department was established on May 18, 1981, following the official elimination of the Office of the City Marshal. This change in the law enforcement structure included appointing a Chief of Police and led to the creation of the Arcola Police Department as outlined in Ordinance No. 4.

141

Ordinance No. 22 abolished the Police Department and reinstated the Office of City Marshal for the City of Arcola on September 17, 1984. However, city officials again eliminated the Office of City Marshal with the enactment of Ordinance 4/1986. The Arcola Police Department was reestablished on February 4, 1997, under Ordinance No. 02-04-97. Additionally, the department received its first official seal on November 18, 1997, as noted in Ordinance No. 11-21-1997.

Strategically located in the heart of the city, the Police Department ensures quick and convenient access to all neighborhoods and communities. The Arcola Police Department is committed to protecting the lives, homes, and properties of the residents of Arcola.

The department aims to serve all citizens by responding to calls for police service, enforcing state and local laws, conducting preventive patrol activities, performing criminal investigations, promoting traffic safety, and apprehending criminal and traffic offenders. The core values of the Arcola Police Department include preserving human life, integrity, professionalism, and service. The department employees and chaplains are all dedicated to serving the community through the divisions outlined below.

The Patrol Division

The Patrol Division is the backbone of the Arcola Police Department, available twenty-four hours a day, seven days a week. This division is responsible for being the first responders to all calls for police service in the city. It consists of full-time officers, reserve officers, and a patrol sergeant. In 2023, the police department logged over 12,000 calls for service in the Computer Aided Dispatch System.

Administrative Division

The Administration Division is made up of sworn officers who fulfill various support roles, including Crime Prevention and Analysis, Accreditation, Property and Evidence Custodian, Evidence Detection, and Training Officer. The administrative staff consists of one patrol lieutenant and the Chief of Police.

In the growing city of Arcola, additional staffing and equipment within the Police Department are needed to enhance the effectiveness of public services.

Fresno Fire and Rescue

Fresno Fire and Rescue has been serving the City of Arcola and its surrounding communities since 1956, covering an area of approximately 37.2 square miles. The department responds to a variety of emergency calls, catering to around 30,000 residents. In early 2020, Fresno Fire and Rescue reorganized to operate under Fort Bend County Emergency Services District No. 7.

As a career department, it is managed by a Board of Commissioners and their consultants, while Chief Anthony Bates and the paid staff handle day-to-day operations. The department operates two fire engines 24/7 to provide coverage and mutual aid to neighboring communities.

Fresno Fire responds to over 2,500 calls for service each year. Additionally, the department plans to transition from essential life support to advanced life support protocols by the end of the year, which will greatly benefit residents during medical emergencies.

1834 W Sycamore, Fresno, Texas 77545

Emergency Services Districts

Emergency Services Districts (ESDs) are established under the Texas Constitution, Article 3, Section 48-e, and Chapter 775 of the Texas Health and Safety Code. ESDs function as political subdivisions of the State of Texas and are authorized to support or provide local emergency services. These services may include emergency medical

assistance, ambulance services, rural fire prevention and control, and other emergency services as permitted by the Texas Legislature. ESDs have the authority to collect sales and use taxes and/or property taxes to fund these services.

Fort Bend County Emergency Services District No. 7 (FBCESD 7) is a political subdivision of Texas that serves as a taxing district to support emergency services. Established in 2017, its Fire Department protects and serves around 30,000 residents and workers within 37.2 square miles of the district, primarily covering the greater Fresno area of Fort Bend County.

OakBend Medical Center

OakBend Medical Center, known initially as Polly Ryon Memorial Hospital, was established in 1947. A group of public-spirited citizens, including A.P. George and Mamie E. George, recognized the need for a hospital in Fort Bend County and decided to establish it. The hospital was built on land donated by Mr. and Mrs. A.P. George and opened on January 15, 1950, with fifty-one fully equipped beds. During its early years, the hospital operated during a time of racial segregation, meaning Black people were often denied access to the same healthcare facilities as white people. However, the hospital began serving Black patients in 1964 following the Civil Rights Act of 1964, which outlawed segregation in public places.

Over the years, OakBend has grown and expanded its services. Key expansions included a new patient wing in 1957 and further additions in 1962-1963, such as a physical therapy department, a surgery and recovery room, and a complete obstetrical department. In 1969, another wing was added, including a coronary care unit and a chapel donated by Mr. and Mrs. August Myers. In 1986, a new 185-bed facility replaced the original building to serve the community's needs better.

Today, OakBend Medical Center has two primary locations in Richmond, Fort Bend County: the Jackson Street Hospital at 1705 Jackson Street, and the Williams Way Hospital Campus at 22003 Southwest Freeway. Both campuses provide a wide range of healthcare services, including emergency services with a No Wait Emergency Room, cardiopulmonary services, medical imaging, intensive care, labor and delivery, neonatal intensive care (NICU), physical therapy, rehabilitation, a skilled nursing facility, a senior behavioral health unit, a sleep lab, and stroke services.

OakBend strongly connects to Fort Bend County, offering essential healthcare services, collaborating with local organizations, and participating in community health initiatives. As a nonprofit organization, OakBend is committed to reinvesting surplus revenue into its facilities and services, ensuring that all patients receive exceptional care, regardless of their ability to pay. The hospital also provides a financial assistance program based on income and federal guidelines to support those in need. This commitment to delivering high-quality, compassionate care has earned OakBend Medical Center the reputation of being a *charity hospital.*

OakBend Medical Center is located within Fort Bend County and benefits residents of Arcola. The center offers comprehensive healthcare services, including emergency care, cardiology, neurology, obstetrics, and more. OakBend's dedication to serving the community ensures that individuals from Arcola and surrounding areas receive high-quality, compassionate healthcare.

Transportation
Fort Bend Transit

Fort Bend Transit was established in 2005 to connect urban and rural areas in Fort Bend County without increasing taxpayer burden. Its mission is to provide safe, efficient public transportation with high quality service.

Fort Bend Transit offers around 392,000 annual passenger trips within Fort Bend and Harris Counties through Demand Response and Commuter Park and Ride services. Demand Response provides curb-to-curb rides across Fort Bend County, while Commuter Park and Ride serves the Texas Medical Center and Greenway Plaza from three locations in Rosenberg and Sugar Land. Services operate on weekdays, excluding county holidays.

Arcola Railways

Today, Arcola, Texas, is served by two major railroads: Union Pacific Railroad and BNSF Railway. Union Pacific operates the former Missouri Pacific line, which has been a key part of the region's rail infrastructure since its acquisition in 1982. BNSF Railway, formed in 1995 through the merger of Burlington Northern and Santa Fe Railways, also operates in the area, intersecting with Union Pacific's tracks. Together, these railroads play a vital role in freight transportation, connecting Arcola to broader national and regional networks.

Velasco Road

Early settlers called the old wagon trail Velasco Road which expanded towards Almeda and was called No. 19, 45, and 288. In 1924, the road was paved with gravel. In 1939, Velasco Road was designated as State Highway 288 (SH 288).

State Highway 288

State Highway 288 (SH 288) was designated on September 26, 1939, renumbering the portion of State Highway 19 that ran south of downtown Houston. On August 1, 1962, SH 288 was extended to Farm to Market Road 1495 (FM 1495).

On June 25, 1981, SH 288 was rerouted from Interstate 45 (I-45) to MacGregor Way in Houston, following a new freeway. Previously, the route traveled south along Almeda Road in Houston, passing through Arcola and near Houston Southwest Airport before reaching Bonney.

On December 14, 1981, the entire segment of SH 288 from US 90 Alternate southward was transferred to Farm to Market Road 521 (FM 521) and Spur 300, as SH 288 was moved onto the new freeway from US 90 Alternate to Spur 300. The route continued east through downtown Angleton and southeast until it reached Freeport. The original section of the highway is now part of County Road 543 and Farm to Market Road 523 (FM 523).

Almeda Road

Before State Highway 288 (SH 288) was established, the road running through Arcola was called Almeda Road. This name dates back to the early 1880s and is derived from the nearby community of Almeda. Dr. Willis King played a significant role in promoting the development of the Almeda area during this time and named the community after his daughter, Almeda King.

The community of Almeda, Texas, was officially established in 1892. Investors from Illinois purchased land near a pre-Civil War railroad line. They laid out the town, initially marketing it as a citrus farming community, which reflected the area's early economic activities.

Farm to Market Road 521

Farm to Market Road 521 (FM 521) is an important route connecting Houston to Palacios in Southeast Texas. The road passes through several communities, including Arcola. FM 521 was officially designated on July 9, 1945, and it is one of the longest farm-to-market roads in Texas, stretching nearly 95 miles.

The route follows the former right-of-way of the Houston Tap and Brazoria Railway, which was constructed in 1858. This railway significantly contributed to the region's development, including the Arcola Plantation.

Texas State Highway 6

Texas State Highway 6 was established on April 4, 1917, as one of the original twenty-five state highways proposed in Texas. This vital route runs through Arcola, Texas, and extends from the Texas-Oklahoma state line to the northwest of Galveston. In the Houston area, it is commonly known as the Old Galveston Highway.

Over the years, SH 6 has experienced several routing changes and expansions to accommodate increasing traffic and improve safety. Initially, it followed the King of Trails Highway. It later incorporated sections of US 75 and US 77. Today, SH 6 passes through various communities, including Arcola, and is a significant regional thoroughfare.

Houston Southwest Airport

Houston Southwest Airport, located at 503 McKeever Road, is a publicly accessible airport privately owned by James Griffith, Jr. It was established in 1976 and spans an area of 165 acres. The airport has one asphalt runway (Runway 9/27) that is 5,002 feet long. In addition, it features 24 hangars and 39 T-hangars for aircraft storage. The airport supports a variety of operations, including general aviation, air taxi services, and occasional military flights.

The Briscoe Canal System

The Briscoe Canal System was established in 1941 by private investor Bob Briscoe and the Briscoe Irrigation Company. In addition to the canal system, they constructed the Briscoe River Plant Pump Station, located south of Missouri City. The primary purpose of this system was to provide irrigation for rice cultivation in Brazoria County. Bob Briscoe and his company were granted water rights to the Brazos River by the State of Texas; a privilege they maintained until the Brazos River Authority acquired the Briscoe Canal System in December 1967.

The Gulf Coast Water Authority manages the Briscoe Canal System. Several planned improvements include upgrades to the electrical service, routine maintenance, canal operations enhancements, and initiatives to increase water resiliency.

These efforts are intended to improve the system's functionality and efficiency. The goal is to enhance the overall performance and reliability of the Briscoe Canal System, benefiting all stakeholders.

Chocolate Bayou

Chocolate Bayou is a freshwater river flowing southeast and emptying into Chocolate Bay. Its watershed includes the cities of Alvin, Arcola, Manvel, and the Village of Iowa Colony. The Texas Commission on Environmental Quality (TCEQ) has been implementing projects to reduce bacteria levels in the bayou, aiming to improve water quality and enhance recreational safety.

The Chocolate Bayou Watershed Master Drainage Study focuses on evaluating drainage needs and creating a comprehensive improvement plan to enhance the overall drainage system, ultimately reducing flooding risks in the Chocolate Bayou area. This detailed analysis covers a 275-acre region and includes the design of roadways, drainage systems, and utilities. Several stormwater detention ponds have been planned to effectively manage stormwater and mitigate flooding. The study also examines the storm drainage system to optimize its performance and minimize street ponding. The Chocolate Bayou Watershed Master Drainage Study is an ongoing project that aims to secure the necessary approvals and permits from various agencies to ensure compliance and successful implementation.

155

Infrastructure Improvements

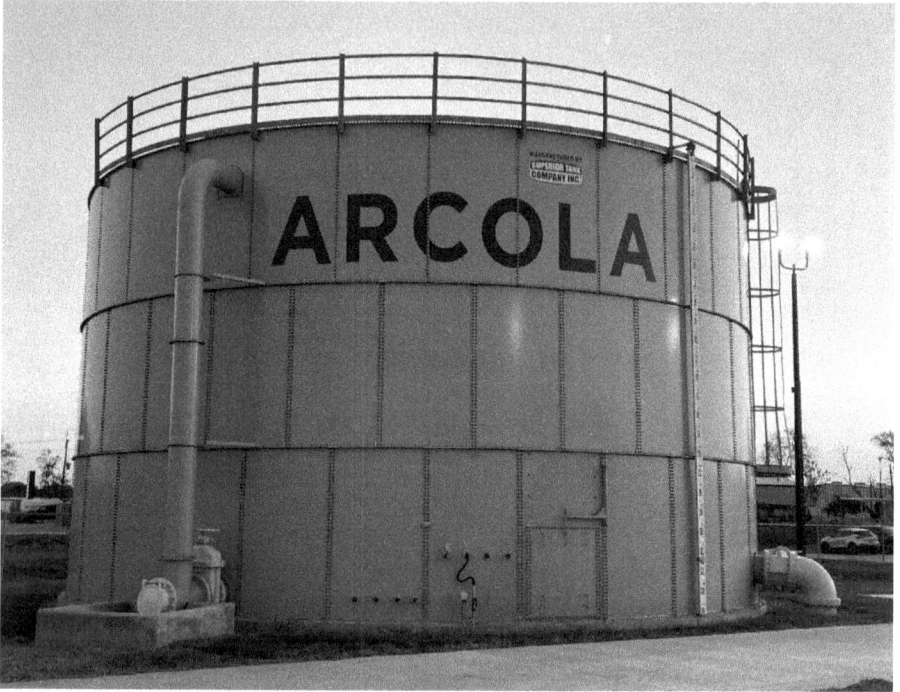

Water Treatment Plant

The Arcola Water Treatment Plant, completed on April 19, 2023, represents a significant advancement for the community. It aims to provide a reliable public water supply for residents who previously depended on backyard wells and septic tanks. This project is a collaborative effort among the Fort Bend Fresh Water Supply District No. 1, Fort Bend County, the City of Arcola, and Fort Bend County Municipal Utility District No. 141. It features a 325,000-gallon storage tank that serves approximately 750 connections in Arcola and the nearby Fresno area. This initiative is part of Arcola's comprehensive infrastructure improvement strategy, with plans to eventually include an additional water plant to meet increasing demand.

Waste Water Treatment Plant

The Arcola Wastewater Treatment Plant is a testament to the city of Arcola's unwavering commitment to public health and environmental stewardship. Established in the mid-20th century, this facility has evolved through decades of technological advancements and expansions. From its humble beginnings with basic treatment processes to its modern-day innovations in sustainability and advanced purification, the plant has played a vital role in ensuring clean water for the community. This narrative chronicles the journey of the Arcola Wastewater Treatment Plant, highlighting the town's dedicated efforts to manage wastewater effectively and protect the local environment.

In the early 20th century, Arcola faced challenges with untreated sewage affecting public health and local water bodies. Recognizing the need for effective wastewater management, the community established a wastewater treatment facility in the 1950s. The plant utilized preliminary treatment to screen out large debris and sedimentation tanks to allow solid particles to settle. The sludge settled at the bottom was treated through anaerobic digestion or disposed of in landfills. This foundational phase demonstrated Arcola's commitment to addressing wastewater issues and protecting local water bodies.

The 1970s brought about significant changes with the passage of the Clean Water Act. This legislation imposed stricter regulations, prompting Arcola to adopt secondary treatment processes. The activated sludge system was introduced, allowing for the aeration of wastewater and encouraging the growth of beneficial microorganisms that consumed organic pollutants. This upgrade significantly improved water quality and ensured compliance with new standards.

As Arcola continued to grow, the wastewater treatment plant needed to expand its capacity. In the 1990s, the plant underwent significant upgrades to handle the increasing volume of wastewater. Tertiary treatment methods, such as advanced filtration and chemical treatments, were introduced to ensure the removal of finer particles and dissolved contaminants. These efforts underscored Arcola's dedication to meeting and exceeding regulatory standards while protecting local water resources.

In the 2000s, the Arcola Wastewater Treatment Plant embraced modern technologies to enhance its capabilities further. The plant adopted membrane bioreactors (MBRs) and ultraviolet (UV) disinfection, significantly improving the removal of fine particles, microorganisms, and pathogens. The city also implemented sustainability initiatives, focusing on energy efficiency, renewable energy sources, and water reuse programs.

In 2009, Layne Christensen Co. began construction on an upgrade to the plant after winning a competitive bid from Brown and Gay Engineering. The project included the construction of new headworks, an in-ground aeration basin, a clarifier, a sludge pump, a chlorine basin, and all supporting piping. Components of the original facility were redesigned and repurposed, with the original racetrack-style plant reconfigured as a digester and the original clarifier repurposed as a thickener. The new plant featured automated grit removal, a mechanical bar screen, and fine air diffusers, significantly improving performance. The project was completed by January 21, 2010.

In 2023, Arcola applied for an upgrade to increase the plant's capacity to 0.95 million gallons per day (MGD). This project aims to accommodate the area's growing population and industrial activities. Additionally, the city plans to expand its capacity further, adopt cutting-edge treatment technologies, and integrate renewable energy sources. These initiatives demonstrate Arcola's commitment to sustainable and effective wastewater management.

In addition to the plant upgrades, Arcola undertook a project to upgrade the Arcola Wastewater Pumping Station (WWPS) and replace the Arcola Force Main (FM). With a budget of $690,000, this project involved replacing both pumps to maintain the 0.17 MGD capacity, replacing 1,300 linear feet of 4" FM and upgrading all electrical and mechanical components, piping assets, and the HVAC system. This upgrade, completed as part of WSSC Water's Asset Management Program, ensured the continued reliability of the wastewater system for approximately 130 households in the Arcola area.

By 2024, Arcola's wastewater treatment plant continued to lead in innovation. The plant introduced advanced treatment technologies, such as anaerobic digestion for energy recovery and nutrient removal processes to reduce nitrogen and phosphorus levels. Rigorous environmental monitoring ensured compliance with regulatory standards and protected local water resources. Community engagement remained a priority, with educational programs and public tours raising awareness about wastewater treatment and environmental protection.

The Arcola Wastewater Treatment Plant is more than just an infrastructure facility. It symbolizes the city's dedication to innovation, sustainability, and the well-being of its community. Through decades of progress and continuous improvement, Arcola has shown that with determination and vision, it is possible to protect public health, preserve the environment, and ensure a bright future for generations to come.

Farm-to-Market Road 521 Expansion
FM 521 from FM 2234 to State Highway 6

The Texas Department of Transportation (TxDOT) is in the process of widening and improving approximately 5.3 miles of Farm-to-Market Road 521 (FM 521) from FM 2234 to State Highway 6. The project aims to add capacity, enhance mobility and traffic safety, and bring the roadway up to current design standards by December 2025.

The expansion will convert FM 521 from a two-lane undivided roadway into a four-lane divided roadway, complete with a median and designated turn lane. Additionally, the project will include accommodation for pedestrians and cyclists, such as a sidewalk and a shared-use lane, as well as the construction of an overpass at Broadway Street to manage increased traffic volumes.

FM 521 from County Road 56 to State Highway 6

The Texas Department of Transportation (TxDOT) is working with the Fort Bend County Engineering Department to widen and improve FM 521 from County Road 56 to State Highway 6. This project aims to enhance mobility, reduce regional congestion, and improve safety by updating the roadway to meet current design standards by March 3, 2026.

The improvements will transform FM 521 from a two-lane undivided roadway into a four-lane divided roadway featuring medians and turn lanes. Additionally, a 10-foot-wide path will be constructed along the east side of FM 521 to accommodate pedestrians and bicyclists. A grade-separated bridge will replace the existing at-grade crossing at the railroad tracks, further enhancing safety.

TxDOT also plans to install five new traffic signals and replace two existing signals at designated locations. The project will involve replacing two bridges over the Briscoe Canal and Juliff Canal, as well as constructing six detention ponds. Approximately sixty-five acres of additional right-of-way will be needed for the project, and one commercial structure, Campbell Concrete and Materials, may need to be relocated.

Historical and Notable Subdivisions

Arcola has a rich history and is home to several historical and notable subdivisions rooted in Abstracts 25 (David Fitzgerald Survey), 31 (William Hall Survey), 170 (Manuel Escalero Survey), and 352 (I&GN Railroad Survey), which together formed the foundation for community development, family homesteads, and civic institutions throughout the city's history.These communities reflect the city's growth from rural settlement to organized municipality. Their legacy continues to shape Arcola's cultural identity and civic landscape.

Historical and Notable Subdivisions

Arcola's subdivisions are more than lines on a plat map; they are living records of how farmland, rail corridors, and family homesteads evolved into organized communities. Each filing reflects a moment in time when landowners, developers, and families reshaped the landscape, leaving behind a paper trail that tells the story of settlement, resilience, and change.

The earliest plats, such as Arcola Farms in the Escalero Survey and Minnequa Gardens in the I&GN Survey, reveal the agricultural backbone of the city. These tracts were carved from working farmland, often tied to railroad access, and they anchored families who sustained Arcola long before incorporation. Mid-century filings like Arcola Heights and Pinedale Manor show the gradual shift toward smaller residential lots, reflecting demographic changes and the beginnings of suburban influence.

By the late 20th century, subdivisions such as Plantation Oaks marked a new era of planned neighborhoods, signaling Arcola's transition from scattered rural tracts to cohesive residential communities. More recent filings, including Post Oak Place, Post Oak Pointe, and Reverie Ranch, illustrate how national builders and local developers alike continue to shape the city's identity, blending modern construction with historic land surveys.

Taken together, these subdivisions form a layered archive of Arcola's growth. They document not only the physical transformation of land but also the social and cultural forces that defined the city, from farming families and educators to developers and civic leaders. To study them is to trace the evolution of Arcola itself, a community rooted in history yet continually adapting to new generations.

Arcola Farms

Arcola Farms was platted as Arcola's first subdivision on May 22, 1935. The plat was filed for record with the Fort Bend County clerk's office on July 9, 1935. The 290.25 acres of land in the Southern part of the Manuel Escalero Survey was surveyed and platted by Arthur H. Jungman and Civil Engineer J. Frank Thompson, Surveyor. Arcola Farms Subdivision has a long, rich history and has been a key component to the community's existence in Fort Bend County over the years. The Manuel Escalero Survey originally consisted of 2569.68 acres.

Arcola Heights Addition

Arcola Heights Addition was established in 1954 by J.E. Kutscher and Harry V. Dulick. Charles Schultz, Licensed Surveyor, surveyed 86.7 acres in the Manuel Escalero Survey in February 1954. The survey was filed and recorded with the Fort Bend County clerk on April 26, 1954.

Arcola Junction

Platted in 1968 within the Barnett Survey (Abstract 7), reflecting proximity to rail lines.

Arcola Townsite

Core civic plat tied to Freedmen's community origins. Incorporated January 17, 1981.

Lowman Ranch

Approved in 2025. Located in the Thomas Barnett Survey (Abstract 7). Developer: Lowman Ranch, Ltd.

Minnequa Gardens

Minnequa Gardens is a small, historic subdivision located within the City of Arcola, tied to the I&GN Railroad Survey (Abstract 352). Platted in the mid-20th century, it reflects the rural residential character of Arcola's early growth, with lots ranging from modest homesteads to larger tracts, such as the nearly 10-acre parcel at 603 Howell Street. Unlike the master-planned communities that later defined Arcola's ETJ, Minnequa Gardens was recorded under traditional clerk filings and appears in property records by legal description rather than marketing name. Its presence underscores the layered development of Arcola, where early plats, such as Minnequa Gardens, coexist with later subdivisions, including Pinedale Manor and Gulfview Acres, anchoring the city's transition from agricultural landholdings to residential neighborhoods.

Post Oak Place

Platted under Plat No. 20170149. Located in Barnett Survey (Abstract 7).

Pinedale Manor Subdivision

Pinedale Manor Subdivision, established in 1969 by J.E. Kutscher, was originally rice fields before its development. Professional Engineer Henry Steinkamp, Jr. surveyed 85.85 acres of property in the Manuel Escalero Survey in March 1969. The Fort Bend Commissioner's Court approved the survey on March 17, 1969, and it was filed with the Fort Bend County clerk on March 20, 1969, and recorded on April 11, 1969. The first houses in Pinedale Manor were built around 1972. Over the years, the neighborhood has continued to develop, with new homes being added to provide affordable housing options for residents.

Plantation Oaks

In 1977, Plantation Ventures, Inc. acquired a tract of land in the Thomas Barnett Survey, Abstract 7, with the goal of reselling it and implementing mutual, beneficial restrictions under a comprehensive plan for the improvement of all the lands in the tract and future owners. The record was filed and signed on March 30, 1977.

Plantation Oaks is a picturesque residential community located in Arcola, Texas. Developed by Plantation Ventures, Inc., starting in 1989, this neighborhood seamlessly blends modern amenities with spacious living. The single-family homes in Plantation Oaks are typically situated on generous lots, often around 1 acre or more, providing ample space for families to enjoy comfortable and stylish living environments.

Whisper South

Approved in 2025, plat filed under Instrument No. 2025012347. Located in Barnett Survey (Abstract 7). Developed by D.R. Horton. Jurisdiction: City of Arcola.

Arcola Municipal Management District

Arcola Municipal Management District No. 1 (City + ETJ overlap). Special-purpose district created to finance infrastructure and support development within city limits and adjacent areas.

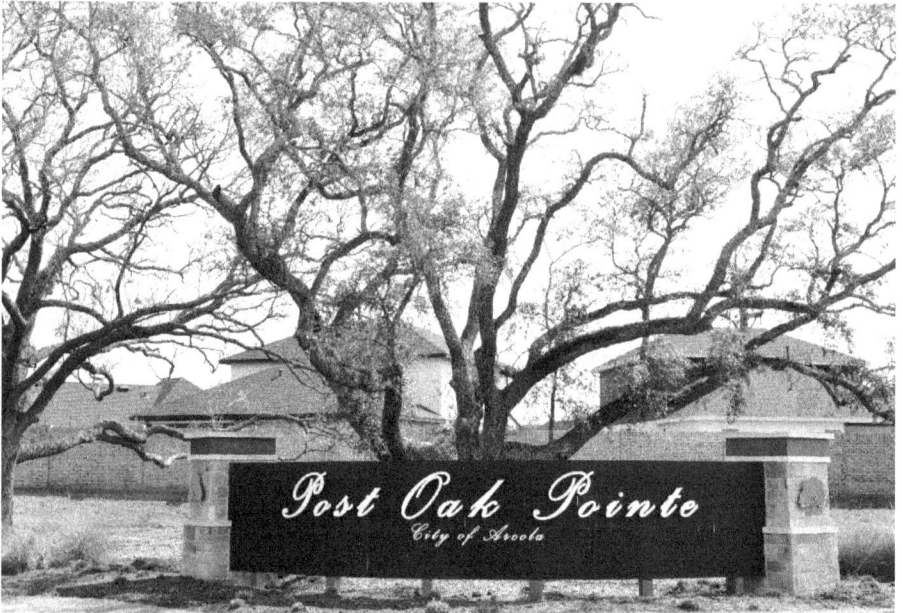

Post Oak Pointe

Post Oak Pointe is a new master-planned community developed by D.R. Horton on 225.9 acres in the Moses Shipman and Thomas Barnett Surveys. It offers a range of single-story and two-story homes with traditional farmhouse elevations (2019).

Reverie Ranch

Reverie Ranch is a new development currently undergoing multiple construction projects to enhance 131.4 acres of land in the David Fitzgerald and Manuel Escalero Surveys. This includes the installation of a lift station and detention facilities. These infrastructure improvements are essential to support the growth of the community. Clearing of the land began on September 10, 2025.

Notable ETJ Subdivisions

Beyond Arcola's incorporated limits lies its extraterritorial jurisdiction (ETJ), a wide band of land where Fort Bend County filings shaped communities that orbit the city but remain outside its municipal authority. These subdivisions are vital to understanding Arcola's growth because they show how developers, families, and builders extended the city's footprint without formally entering its boundaries.

Early ETJ plats such as House Plantation and Gulfview Acres reveal the agricultural and railroad heritage that defined the area long before suburban expansion. Mid-century filings like Skyview Farms and Glenns Village illustrate the persistence of rural residential life, with modest tracts carved from the Barnett and Escalero surveys. By the late 20th century, larger developments such as Southern Colony and Teal Run marked the arrival of master-planned communities, reflecting the influence of national builders and the growing demand for affordable housing near Houston's southern corridor.

In the 21st century, subdivisions like Barnett Woods, Meadowvale, and One Oak Chase continued this trend, blending suburban design with historic survey lines. More recent filings, Caldwell, Charleston Heights, Glendale Lakes, and Glendale Lakes North, demonstrate how the ETJ remains a hub of active development, with national builders investing heavily in tracts that carry Arcola addresses but fall under county jurisdiction.

Taken together, these ETJ subdivisions form a parallel archive to the city's own plats. They document how Arcola's identity extends beyond its legal boundaries, shaped by families, developers, and institutions who contributed to the region's growth while remaining outside municipal incorporation.

Gulfview Acres

The Gulfview Acres subdivision was established in 1957 by J.E. Kutscher and Harry V. Dulick. Consulting Engineer Steinkamp & Bickham surveyed 70.33 acres in the Manuel Escalero Survey in April 1956. The survey was filed and recorded with the Fort Bend County clerk on December 30, 1957. *This subdivision was platted in Arcola, Texas, before the boundaries were drawn in 1981 to incorporate the unincorporated township as a city.

One Oak Chase Subdivision

One Oak Chase Subdivision was established in 1981 when Laura Dietz Fenn sold the last remaining piece of land belonging to the descendants of David Fitzgerald for development. The subdivision features a mix of single-family homes and mobile homes, offering a variety of living options.

The subdivision is situated on Fenn Road, which serves as the boundary between the Thomas Barnett and David Fitzgerald surveys in Arcola. This area is part of Stephen F. Austin's Old Three Hundred settlements from 1824.

Barnett Estates

Filed in 1982 within the Barnett Survey (Abstract 7). Jurisdiction: ETJ.

Barnett Woods

Filed in 2001 within the Barnett Survey (Abstract 7). Larger lots, rural character. Jurisdiction: ETJ.

Blue Ridge West / Ridgewood Estates

Blue Ridge West / Ridgewood Estates (1980s–1990s, ETJ)
Phased suburban plats filed late 20th century. Jurisdiction: ETJ.

Caldwell

Developed by D.R. Horton beginning in 2023. Located in Barnett Survey (Abstract 31). Jurisdiction: ETJ.

Charleston Heights

Developed by Legend Homes beginning in 2021. Located in Barnett Survey (Abstract 170). Jurisdiction: ETJ.

Commercial Plats

Several small commercial and industrial tracts along Highway 6 and FM 521 were platted under generic names, including *Arcola Business Park* and *FM 521 Commercial Reserve.* These filings typically cover strip centers, warehouses, or service facilities. Each plat carries its own instrument number and filing date. Jurisdiction varies: some lie within the City of Arcola limits, others in the ETJ.

Fenn Road Lot Splits

One-off filings along Fenn Road created small residential tracts without formal subdivision names. Recorded under individual instrument numbers in Barnett and Fitzgerald Surveys. Jurisdiction: ETJ.

Glendale Lakes

A master-planned community initially developed by Saratoga Homes, later phases by KB Home and Meritage Homes. Located in the I&GN RR CO Survey (Abstract 352). Jurisdiction: ETJ. Multiple phases filed separately, each with its own instrument number and filing date.

Glendale Lakes North

Extension of Glendale Lakes, developed by KB Home. Located in I&GN RR CO Survey (Abstract 352). Jurisdiction: ETJ.

Glenns Village

Modest subdivision platted in the 1970s along the Fenn Road corridor within Arcola's extraterritorial jurisdiction. Situated in the Thomas Barnett Survey (Abstract 7), with possible overlap into the David Fitzgerald Survey (Abstract 25). Jurisdiction: ETJ.

House Plantation

Originally part of the House Plantation estate, platted in 1927 within the Barnett Survey (Abstract 7). Jurisdiction: ETJ.

Meadowvale

Filed in 1992. Located in Barnett Survey (Abstract 7). Jurisdiction: ETJ.

Riley's Point

Approved in 2025, plat filed under Instrument No. 2025012346. Located in Barnett Survey (Abstract 7). Jurisdiction: ETJ.

Sienna Plantation Villages

Johnson Development Corporation platted Sienna Plantation in multiple villages beginning in the late 1990s. Villages overlapping Arcola's ETJ include Waters Lake, Shipman's Landing, and Bees Creek. Each village filed separately between 1997 and 2005. Surveys include William Stafford and Moses Shipman (Abstract 89/86). Jurisdiction: ETJ.

Skyview Farms

Platted in 1957, Fort Bend County Clerk records Volume 15, Page 89. Jurisdiction: ETJ.

Southern Colony

Developed by D.R. Horton and others beginning in the 2000s. Each section filed separately in Fort Bend County Clerk records. Located in Barnett Survey (Abstract 7). Jurisdiction: ETJ.

Teal Run

Developed by Royce Homes and others in the 1990s. Each section filed separately in Fort Bend County Clerk records. Located in Moses Shipman Survey (Abstract 89/86). Jurisdiction: ETJ.

Arcola Misnamed but Never Erased

Properties in Arcola often bear Rosharon or Fresno mailing addresses because the U.S. Postal Service assigns ZIP codes and routing based on distribution centers rather than municipal boundaries. Since Arcola is a small city, its postal routes overlap with those of larger neighboring communities, which means that even land located firmly inside Arcola's city limits may list Rosharon or Fresno as the mailing city. This postal overlap, however, does not alter jurisdictional realities.

Municipal boundaries, taxing authority, and school district assignments remain tied to Arcola itself. For researchers and archivists, the distinction is critical because mailing addresses can easily be misinterpreted when reconstructing property histories or family records. This confusion is reinforced when funeral programs, obituaries, and business documents repeat the postal city designation, obscuring the true civic identity of Arcola families and institutions.

In legal contexts, too, mislabeling properties as belonging to Rosharon or Fresno can create confusion, particularly in disputes where jurisdiction must be clearly established. Recognizing that postal routing reflects logistics rather than governance helps restore clarity, and it underscores the importance of relying on deeds, plats, and appraisal records as authoritative sources. At the same time, preserving Arcola's distinct identity in historical and genealogical documentation ensures that the community's agency is not lost within the shadow of its larger neighbors, reinforcing the dignity of residents who have long identified with Arcola as their home.

Yet postal routing is only one way Arcola's identity can be obscured; a more significant shift occurs when neighboring cities annex portions of its land. Annexation does not erase the property lines themselves. Those boundaries are set by the original survey, plat, or deed and remain permanently recorded in county deed records. A tract carved from a survey will always keep its acreage and survey reference, no matter what happens later.

What annexation changes is the jurisdictional boundary, meaning which city government has authority over the land. When a larger city annexes part of Arcola, the land is legally placed inside that city's limits for purposes of taxes, utilities, and ordinances. The property lines stay exactly the same, but the government in charge shifts, meaning the land remains Arcola in origin even as jurisdiction changes.

It is important to understand that even after annexation, the land still comes from Arcola. Its survey, deed chain, and historical identity remain tied to Arcola's geography. Annexation does not rewrite that origin; it only changes who governs the land today. In practice, this means the owner's title and acreage remain intact, but the civic identity is layered: historically Arcola, jurisdictionally another city, creating a layered identity that must be carefully documented to preserve Arcola's place in the historical record.

Where Children Played and Families Built

This photograph, taken along Cooper Lane in Abstract 31 within the Arcola Farms Subdivision, captures a vivid moment in the everyday life of rural Texas families during the late 1950s and early 1960s. The modest homes, built between the 1940s and early 1960s, display the practical architecture of the era, simple gable roofs, wood siding, and unadorned facades that reflected both limited resources and enduring resilience. In front of these houses, children gather in play, their clothing and hairstyles reflecting the fashions of the late 1950s and early 1960s. A parked automobile, typical of that period, further situates the scene in its historical context. Together, the houses and the children embody the lived reality of Arcola Farms: a subdivision that was not only a platted tract but also a community where families carved out space, built lives, and left a legacy that remains part of Arcola's layered history.

Photo courtesy of Richard *Pete* Simon

Legacy Families

Arcola's legacy families built more than homes; they established roots that shaped the community. Through hard work, they sustained farms, raised children, and preserved traditions that carried the town forward. Their presence across generations reflects resilience and continuity, anchoring Arcola's place in Fort Bend County history.

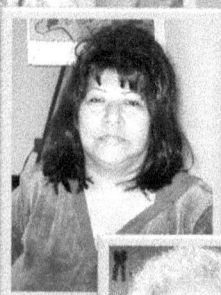

Mary Etta Anderson's Reflections on the Beginnings of the Hearts of Arcola

Back in 2012, I regularly attended senior citizen events at the Mustang Community Center. I enjoyed speaking with the seniors there, learning about their experiences, and hearing their thoughts on the Fort Bend County-sponsored senior programs. One common theme kept coming up was that they wanted more activities and engagement at the Center.

We began brainstorming ideas together, and I asked if they'd be interested in coming to City Hall once a week, provided I could get approval from the County Supervisor overseeing the Mustang Center. They were enthusiastic and agreed.

I reached out to the Supervisor and shared my plan to host the seniors at City Hall weekly. The gatherings would include a light breakfast, lunch on occasion, and always beverages. Those relying on transportation could still use Fort Bend County Metro services. Thankfully, the Supervisor approved the idea, and that's how the *Hearts of Arcola* was born.

Mrs. Doris, their assigned Supervisor, joined them during these visits. The seniors typically came on Tuesdays or Wednesdays, unless there was a conflicting county event. We brought a projector and showed movies they selected, westerns, comedies, cartoons, and more. We also had someone assist with arts and crafts, often themed around upcoming holidays like Valentine's Day, St. Patrick's Day, or Easter. They made baskets, decorated pails, and arranged flowers, often filling them with candy to gift or sell at craft fairs.

For a few weeks, Pastor Perry from Word of Restoration sent someone to lead Bible study sessions, which the seniors appreciated. The city provided free beverages, and someone from the group would bring tacos. Baty's Produce occasionally donated fresh fruit, which I or the

City Secretary would turn into fruit trays. Most of the time, I personally provided lunch.

We also had a computer lab connected to the Fort Bend ISD system, available for citizens without home computers. Some seniors wanted to learn Microsoft Word, and with the help of a volunteer, we arranged lessons. They quickly picked it up, writing letters and sending emails to family members, which thrilled them. Others preferred playing games, and that was perfectly fine too. The joy they found in these activities was heartwarming.

Jay Jurico, owner of the Arcola Feed Store, hosted a Trade Day on the first Saturday of each quarter. People sold everything from livestock to furniture. I asked Jay about a table for the seniors to sell their crafts, and he generously donated one. They sold out every time! At City Hall events, they'd set up their table and sell out again.

As for the money they earned, the City Secretary managed the Hearts of Arcola funds. Once they had enough, the seniors chose how to spend it. I gave them options like field trips, Golden Corral, or Pappadeaux Seafood Kitchen. They usually picked Pappadeaux, and had a wonderful time!

The Hearts of Arcola, captured during Mother's Day Luncheon. Pictured from Left to right: Marie Dove, Mary, [unknown], [unknown], Jacinta Regino Barrios, Miriam Parker, Macy, Bonnie, Mayor Mary Anderson, Doris Steven (Supervisor of the Center), [unknown], Joyce Edison, [unknown], Timothy Johnson

Arcola Legacy Families

Allen
Archie
Austin
Bonner
Boone
Bolts
Breedlove
Brookin
Broussard
Burns
Collier
Cooper
Dade
Davis
Delaney
Duncan
Edison
England
Evans
Faultry
Francis
Fredrick
Gales
Gaston
George (Johnny)
Gibbs
Gibson

Green
Griffin
Hall
Hamilton
Harris
Hayes
Henderson
Herod
Holman
Hubbard
Hudson
Hughes
Jefferson
Jesse
Johnson
Jones
Kerney
Knapp
Lawson
Lincoln
Lundford
Lundy
Qualls
Massie
Matthews
Mitchell
Parker

Posley
Perkins
Petry
Pickett
Pratt
Price
Ramsey
Robinson
Rogers
Senior
Sessum
Simon
Smith
Sosa
Tate
Tribble
Turner
Walker
Warren
Washington
Wells
Whitehead
Wiley
Williams

The Williams Family

James and Phillippe Love Williams

The Williams family is deeply rooted in Arcola, Texas, leaving its mark in the history of the small community. Both James and Phillippe served the Arcola community through faithful dedication to the church and the local education system, exemplifying their service to others. James Williams, an Army veteran, hailed from Dewalt, Texas, and as the father of 12 kids, became an advocate for education, participating in FBISD projects to ensure the youth of Arcola received equitable education and resources. His wife, Phillippe Love Williams, originally from Sandy Point, Texas, was a devoted mother who began working in the FBISD school system only after her last child (#12) completed elementary school. Even after such a late start in the workforce, she worked for 20 years before retiring from FBISD. She was a faithful servant of New Saint Philip Baptist Church until her passing in 2002.

Service to others was a characteristic that was ingrained in the fabric of the Williams family, as it was passed to their kids as well. James and Phillippe raised their twelve children in a cozy, family-oriented home located in Arcola Farms, the city's very first subdivision. The home - the *Trummie Cain Special*; a model named for a local Black musician - was a reminder of the times in which it was built by L.M. Inkley Company, in 1957; owners and developers who built *Properties Exclusively for Colored People*. Despite the times, their home was a nurturing environment, within a community rich in history. James and

Citizen Input

James William and Dr. Bill Payne review the 78-79 ESAA project proposal. To allow maximum citizen input on the plan, the district will hold a second public hearing at 7:30 p.m. tonight in the Blue Ridge Elementary School cafetorium.

Philippe instilled strong values of respect, education, service, and leadership in all of their children. All twelve graduated from high school, and nine of them served in the military, illustrating the family's incredible commitment to service and resilience. Among their children is Dr. Veeda V. Williams, the youngest, who was elected Mayor of the City of Arcola on May 4, 2024. An accomplished educator, U.S. Air Force veteran, and co-founder of Community Express, Inc., Dr. Williams has been championing the youth of Arcola for over thirty years. Her leadership brings the same passion, commitment, and dedication that have been hallmarks of her family's legacy. Guided by a profound understanding of local needs, she envisions a united and thriving city that delivers practical solutions for its residents.

On February 21, 2025, the City of Arcola celebrated its rich history through an Art Dedication honoring Monroe Williams, whose artwork captured the very essence of the people and community of Arcola, Texas, throughout the years. This tribute exemplifies the Williams family's ongoing contributions to the cultural and social fabric of Arcola.

Willie Jean Hayes

Willie Jean Hayes was born in March 1933 in the rural heart of Arcola, Fort Bend County, Texas, the third of nine children born to Will Sessums, a tenant farmer, and Lillie Delaney Sessums, a homemaker and pianist. Their wood-frame house near FM 521 stood within walking distance of Mount Pilgrim Baptist Church.

Her grandparents, George and Mary Delaney, were sharecroppers and church leaders. George served as a deacon, and Mary led the women's prayer circle. Oral history and cemetery geography place them in Mount Pilgrim Baptist Church Cemetery, across from the land they once worked.

By age seven, Willie Jean appeared in the 1940 U.S. Census, living with her siblings: Elnora, James, Martha, Robert, Annie, Lillie Mae, George Jr., and Clara. Her childhood unfolded among cotton fields, rice paddies, and the rhythms of a segregated schoolhouse where she first learned to read, sing, and lead. She was baptized in a galvanized tub behind the church and later taught Sunday School from her family's porch when the sanctuary fell into disrepair.

In the 1950 census, she remained in Arcola as a young adult. She married George Hayes, a fellow congregant and farmhand, and together they raised three children, Henry Jr., Delores, and Thomas Ray. She hosted choir rehearsals and youth Bible study well into the 1990s, long after the church building vanished, but its spirit remained.

Willie Jean served in the Women's Missionary Circle, sang alto in the Mount Pilgrim choir, and taught Sunday School with the same precision she brought to her household. She also signed petitions for school board reform.

According to her own account later in life, Arcola was *a perfect area to move to for work.* The work was cotton, rice, corn, beans, okra, and raising chickens and hogs. Men in the community also worked in the rice fields planting and harvesting, and for ranches raising and grazing livestock such as cattle, sheep, goats, and horses. Transportation in Arcola included the city bus, Trailways line from Houston, which ran three times a day between Houston and Bay City. Residents traveled to Houston and Sugar Land for shopping, hospitals, and entertainment. The local community store, Buster Tripp, stood at the corner of Highway 6 and FM 521.

Her funeral was in 2011. She was laid to rest in Mount Pilgrim Baptist Church Cemetery, across from the land where she was born, prayed, and taught.

She lived where she was born and died where she prayed.

Notable Historical People & Sites

Arcola has a rich history and is home to several notable figures and landmarks. Early settlers and plantation owners shaped the town's beginnings, while freed Black families built churches, businesses, and community institutions that gave the town lasting strength. Historic sites such as the old railroad junction and Arcola's earlier churches preserve these stories, reminding us of the town's role in Texas settlement, agriculture, and community development.

The Rosenberg Post Office at 2103 Avenue G, completed in 1939, holds the distinction of being the first stand-alone post office building in Fort Bend County constructed by the U.S. Treasury Department.

Arcola Postmasters

William D. Dering, February 22, 1869

Discontinued August 12, 1869

(Re-established) Jas. S. Jones, July 22, 1872

Jos. Smart, Jos., April 22, 1873

Discontinued July 11, 1873

Re-established Francis Jueger, June 22, 1874

Green K. Cessna, August 15, 1878

Paul deManade, August 31, 1880

Discontinued January 7, 1884; mail to Duke

Re-established William Wood, April 8, 1897

Discontinued September 14, 1907; mail to Duke

Re-established Peter M. Leishman, October 31, 1911

Lula M. Eilers, December 22, 1913

Frank O. Keir, November 23, 1917

Myrtie E. Thatcher, January 9, 1920

Discontinued November 15, 1920; mail to Iowa Colony

Grady Prestage

Since 1990, Grady Prestage has been a pivotal leader in Fort Bend County, advancing infrastructure, mobility, and community development. Elected to the Commissioners Court in November 1990, he became the first African American commissioner in the county since Thomas Lane Taylor in 1882 during the Reconstruction era. His enduring leadership, marked by seven re-elections, reflects his steadfast commitment to the residents of Precinct 2, which includes Houston, Missouri City, Stafford, Arcola, Needville, Fresno, Thompsons, Juliff, Trammels, Sienna, Riverstone, and Southern Colony.

A civil engineer by profession, Commissioner Prestage, brings significant expertise to county development. He holds a Bachelor's Degree in Civil Engineering from Southern University in Baton Rouge, Louisiana, and is a Registered Professional Engineer in Texas. His technical background has been crucial in shaping infrastructure improvements across Fort Bend County.

Throughout his tenure, Commissioner Prestage has championed numerous initiatives to enhance public resources and mobility. He played a leading role in establishing the Fort Bend County Community Development Department, the Fort Bend County Housing Finance Corporation, and the Fort Bend Toll Road Authority. His efforts have expanded parks, libraries, community centers, and major transportation projects, improving access and quality of life for residents across Precinct 2.

Beyond county affairs, Prestage has held leadership positions in organizations such as the Texas Organization of Black County Commissioners, the National Association of Counties (NACo), and the Texas Association of Counties (TAC). He was appointed by Governor Ann Richards to the Board of Regents for the Lamar University System and the Texas County and District Retirement System, contributing to policies benefiting communities statewide.

Pearl's Chicken Shack

Arcola's Culinary Heartbeat

Pearl Virginia Lawson Bradley was born on July 1, 1919, to Dennis Lawson and Annie Bell Posley. She grew up in a close-knit family as sister to Lillie Mae Lawson Bradley and Elnora Lawson Williams, and later became aunt to James *Jimmy* Lawson Jr. These ties anchored her within Arcola's Black community, where kinship networks connected households to churches, schools, and civic spaces. Pearl eventually married Willie Bradley, and together they became part of the fabric of community life in Fort Bend County.

From the mid-1940s until her passing in 1970, Pearl's name was inseparable from one place: Pearl's Chicken Shack. Nestled near the civic core of Arcola, Texas, within Abstract 170 along the FM 521 corridor, the Shack operated as both a business and a gathering place. Though no deed or business license survives, descendants and longtime residents vividly recall it as a cornerstone of Black social life in mid-century Arcola. Pearl herself is remembered with varying surnames in family accounts; some say Lawson, others Bradley, but all agree on her warmth, her generosity, and her unmatched skill with a cast-iron skillet. Her apron was dusted with flour, her laugh carried across the yard, and her fried chicken, hot biscuits, and sweet tea became legendary across Fort Bend County.

As the Shack grew in reputation, it became more than a place to eat. On Sunday evenings, after church services and sandlot baseball games, neighbors gathered around an outdoor jukebox that spun gospel and rhythm & blues. The yard transformed into a dance floor, a debriefing circle, and a second sanctuary where laughter worked like medicine. Farmhands, schoolchildren, elders, and ball players all found a seat at Pearl's table. According to Veeda Williams, the gatherings were so beloved that *cars were lined up on both sides of the road as far as the eye could see,* a sight that testified to Pearl's role as a civic anchor.

The memories of those nights endure through oral testimony. Monroe Williams recalled plainly, *He would play at Pearl's,* confirming that bluesman Lightnin' Hopkins performed there. In genealogical forums, descendants still write of her biscuits, *better than any restaurant,* and of Sundays when *Miss Pearl fed half the town after church.* Local interviews and church bulletins remember her jukebox, her generosity, and the way she kept a table open for elders as a matter of respect. Extending credit when crops failed, feeding players after doubleheaders, and keeping her doors open to all, Pearl turned her business into a quiet ledger of community care.

Though absent from county archives, her Shack is mapped in memory through descendant storytelling and the lived recollections of those who gathered there.

Pearl passed on September 15, 1970. Yet her legacy endures not in advertisements or deeds, but in the voices that still say her name, in the taste of food remembered decades later, and in the music that once spilled from her jukebox into the Arcola night. Pearl's Chicken Shack became the precursor to later venues like the Sugar Shack, proof that Arcola's tradition of gathering, feeding, and celebrating one another has deep and lasting roots.

The Sugar Shack of Arcola, Texas

A Cultural Beacon of Black Western Life

Ron Alex Mitchell, affectionately known as *Sugar,* was born on September 26, 1946, and became a cherished figure in Arcola, Texas, remembered for his military service, community leadership, and cultural vision. Following his time in uniform, Mitchell emerged as a driving force in Fort Bend County's cultural life.

Located near the FM 521 corridor in Arcola, the Sugar Shack Disco Club operated from 1981 to 1988 as far more than a nightclub—it was a beloved community gathering place and cultural institution. Under Mitchell's charismatic leadership, the Sugar Shack became a regional hub for Black cowboys, trail riders, and country-western dance enthusiasts from across Fort Bend County and greater Houston. The venue bridged Black urban energy with rural western traditions, uniting generations, styles, and stories during a transformative era. In partnership with Nathan Jean Whitaker Sanders, fondly called *Mama Sugar*, Mitchell infused the Sugar Shack with pride, purpose, and celebration of Black western heritage. Together, they offered country-western dance classes, hosted rodeo after-parties, and created a welcoming space that nurtured Black trail-riding communities while spotlighting their contributions to Texas history. It was during this era that Mama Sugar founded the Sugar Shack Trailblazers, a family-oriented riding group registered with the Southwestern Trail Riders Association. Blending horsemanship with cultural education, the Trailblazers often began or ended their rides at the club, where the dance floor pulsed with gospel, blues, and country hits, and the kitchen served soul food so renowned it earned regional acclaim, including a feature in *Gourmet Magazine* for its Juneteenth recipes.

Though the Sugar Shack closed its doors in 1988, its spirit lives on in oral history, in the lore of trail-riding clubs, and in the hearts of those who danced, learned, and found fellowship there. It stands as a modern echo of earlier Arcola institutions like Pearl's Chicken Shack, spaces where food, music, and community turned ordinary nights into enduring memories.

Jake Dove Community Center (1993)
A Legacy of Mentorship in Arcola, Texas

In 1979, Fort Bend County purchased the former Oaklane Elementary School building from Fort Bend Independent School District. The county converted the site into the Arcola Community Center, later designated in official 1980 election documents as the Jake Dove Community Center.

The Jake Dove Community Center, a 4,000-square-foot facility located at 400 Coen Road in Arcola on 3.5 acres, was established in 1993 as a local hub for social services, youth programming, and community support. The center was named in honor of Jake Dove, a respected elder and civic figure whose life embodied the values of mentorship, discipline, and care for future generations.

Jake Dove's life reflects why the community chose to honor him. Born on February 28, 1880, Jake Dove lived to be 101 years old, passing away in January 1982. He resided in Rosharon, Brazoria County, just adjacent to Arcola, and was known throughout Fort Bend County for his quiet leadership and commitment to uplifting young people. While formal records of his professional life are limited, oral history and community memory suggest that Dove was deeply involved in local education, youth guidance, and civic stewardship. His name became synonymous with integrity and service, and the decision to name the center after him was a tribute to his enduring influence.

The center itself operated for years as a multipurpose facility, hosting neighborhood meetings, youth outreach programs, and educational services. In the early 2000s, it was renovated to house the Fort Bend

County Juvenile Justice Alternative Education Program (JJAEP) and the Juvenile Leadership Academy (JLA). These programs served court-assigned and expelled students aged 12 to 17, offering academic remediation, vocational training, and counseling in a structured, supportive environment. The facility included a 4,000-square-foot classroom building, a vocational shop, offices for therapists and probation officers, and a gym for military-style drills and recreation.

Though the center was later repurposed and renamed, its original dedication to Jake Dove remains a powerful symbol of Arcola's values: honoring those who uplift others, investing in youth, and building institutions that reflect the heart of the community. Dove's legacy lives on not just in the name on the door, but in the lives shaped within its walls.

ARCOLA COMMUNITY CENTER

Dedicated To

HONORABLE
GLENN "BAM BAM" SANCO

Council Member

May 19, 2015 ~ July 10, 2018

Glen *Bam Bam* Sanco Community Room

Glen *Bam Bam* Sanco was a towering presence in Arcola, both in stature and in spirit. Known for his kindness, loyalty, and willingness to help anyone in need, Sanco became a fixture of his community. He served two terms on the Arcola City Council, where he was admired for his approachable nature and commitment to representing everyday residents.

Outside of public service, Sanco worked as a tow truck driver, a role that became an extension of his community care. He was known to respond to calls at any hour, helping not only stranded motorists but also law enforcement officers. On December 27, 2018, Sanco demonstrated his character in two separate incidents. First, he stopped to back up a state trooper during a chaotic traffic stop, offering his support and exchanging contact information with the officer. Later that same day, he intervened again when a suspect fled from troopers near FM 521 and Trammel Fresno Road. Sanco tackled the suspect, holding him until officers could make the arrest.

Moments after this act of bravery, Sanco collapsed from what was believed to be a massive heart attack. Despite CPR efforts, he passed away at a local hospital. His death was widely mourned, with tributes pouring in from family, friends, and law enforcement. His wife, Ebony Sanco, remembered him as someone who would do anything for anyone and was *the best person I've known.* His sister Chloe described him as *an angel* whose presence uplifted those around him.

Sanco always dreamed of becoming a police officer, but the responsibilities of providing for his family kept him from pursuing that path. In his final hours, however, he lived out that dream by protecting and assisting troopers in the line of duty.

In 2020, the City of Arcola honored Glen *Bam Bam* Sanco by naming the community room in its city hall after him. Sanco is remembered as a true hero of Arcola, a man whose final acts reflected the values he lived by every day: courage, generosity, and service to others. His legacy continues to inspire, reminding residents of Arcola and beyond that, genuine leadership is not measured only by elected office but by the everyday acts of kindness and bravery that strengthen a community.

Monroe Williams
The Artist

Monroe Williams

Monroe Williams is an Arcola native whose art carries the soul of his hometown in every brushstroke. Raised in the rhythms of rural Texas, he paints what he knows: the quiet dignity of horse-drawn wagons, the strength of laboring hands, and the landscapes that shaped generations. His work doesn't just depict the past; it preserves it, offering a visual archive of lives lived with purpose, humility, and grace.

As a Marine veteran, Williams brings discipline, resilience, and reverence to his creative practice. That sense of duty extends beyond his military service; it's woven into his canvases and his commitment to community. His paintings are more than aesthetic; they're acts of remembrance, tributes to the people and places that shaped him.

Williams has exhibited widely, but his heart remains in Arcola. He's mentored young artists, participated in local initiatives, and helped build a creative culture rooted in heritage and pride. His legacy is not confined to gallery walls; it lives in the stories he tells, the artists he uplifts, and the community he continues to serve.

On February 21, 2025, the City of Arcola honored his contributions by proclaiming February 21, 2025, as Monroe Williams Day. It was more than a ceremonial gesture; it was a recognition of a man whose art bridges generations, whose life reflects the values of service, creativity, and cultural stewardship.

Monroe Williams paints with memory, with meaning, and with love for the land that raised him. His work stands as a living testament to Arcola's past and a beacon for its future.

Doris Mae Dearing Senior

For nearly one hundred years, Doris Mae Dearing Senior stood as a quiet force in the rural life of Fort Bend County. Born on November 14, 1924, in Los Angeles, she grew into a woman whose life was defined not by where she began, but by the community she shaped, the family she nurtured, and the steady presence she carried into every room she entered. Her story is woven into the land, the people, and the memory of the Arcola area, not through headlines or public monuments, but through the everyday acts of service that hold a community together.

Doris was the daughter of Gus and Lilla Mae Dearing, raised in a family that valued work, faith, and responsibility. She carried those values into adulthood when she married Robert Oliver *Bob* Senior on November 3, 1942, her partner in life and the father of her children. Together, they built a family rooted in devotion to each other, to their children, and to the rural community that surrounded them.

Although Doris did not live on Arcola Plantation, she and her husband were connected to the small Catholic church located on the plantation grounds, a place where many rural families gathered for worship. The chapel was part of their spiritual life, but it was not the center of Doris's community identity. Her true presence in the community emerged elsewhere, in the everyday work that touched people's lives far beyond Sunday mornings.

For years, the Senior family operated a small agricultural supply store remembered by the community as the Senior Country Feed Store, a place where ranchers, farmers, and horse owners along Highway 6 came for feed, hay, tack, seed, and the everyday necessities of rural life. It was the kind of store that did not need a sign to be known;

people simply knew where it was, who ran it, and that they would be treated with honesty and respect.

It was through the Senior Country Feed Store that Doris became part of the heartbeat of the community. Day after day, she greeted neighbors, offered help, shared conversation, and provided the kind of quiet support that defines rural life. People came for supplies, but they also came because they trusted her, because she was steady, kind, and always ready to lend a hand.

Doris herself was known for her gentle strength. A devout Catholic, she lived her faith through action. She cared for others *with a prayer and a smile*, a phrase that captures both her spirit and her resilience. She was the person families called when they needed help, the caregiver who stepped in with compassion, the neighbor who offered comfort without hesitation. Her kindness was not loud or showy; it was steady, dependable, and deeply felt by those who knew her.

As Fort Bend County changed, as fields gave way to subdivisions and the old agricultural corridor transformed, Doris remained a living link to the history of the land. She represented a time when families knew one another by name, when stores like the Senior Country Feed Store were lifelines, and when the rhythms of rural life shaped the identity of the community.

Doris lived to be 99 years old, passing away on July 6, 2024. She was preceded in death by her husband, her son Robert Jr., her grandson Jefforey, her parents, and her siblings. She leaves behind her children, seven grandchildren, twenty-three great-grandchildren, and extended family who cared for her with the same devotion she once offered to others. Her life was honored with a memorial visitation in Alvin and a Mass at Sacred Heart Catholic Church in Manvel, a reflection of the faith that guided her from childhood to her final days.

Her legacy is not measured in buildings or plaques, but in the people she touched, the community she supported, and the history she carried forward. In the story of Arcola and the surrounding countryside, Doris Mae Dearing Senior remains a figure of quiet power, a woman whose life, family, and service form a chapter of Fort Bend County's history that deserves to be preserved, honored, and remembered.

The Broussards

The Broussard family is one of the rooted Black rural lineages that helped shape the agricultural community of Arcola, Texas, throughout the twentieth century. Their story reflects the lived experience of families who built their lives on the land—working, raising children, serving their community, and maintaining continuity across generations even when official histories overlooked them. They are one of Arcola's pillar families, remembered for their deep roots, public service, and legacy.

The Broussards trace their origins to Louisiana, part of the westward movement of Black Creole families who migrated into Texas seeking stability and opportunity. By mid-century, the family had established a stable presence in Arcola, connected through marriage, land, and community ties to other long-standing families in the region.

A central figure in the documented lineage is Claude Joseph Broussard Jr. (1932–1980). Born in Houston and raised in Arcola, Claude Jr. was the son of Claude Joseph Broussard Sr. and Ruby Katherine Jackson, linking the Broussards to the Jackson family line. He served in the U.S. Army, worked as a truck driver in the freight industry, and was active in local politics. Claude Jr. passed away on November 30, 1980, at his home on Fenn Road in Arcola.

Claude Jr. married Ruth Faye Delaney in Harris County on June 24, 1956, a union that joined two long-standing regional families and anchored Ruth's presence in Arcola. Ruth became a respected civic leader in her own right, serving as Arcola's precinct judge. Her public service placed the Broussard name directly into the civic record, marking her as one of the few Black rural women in Fort Bend County to hold an official election role during that era. Her leadership was nationally recognized: Ruth Faye Delaney was listed in *Who's Who in American Politics*, Sixth Edition (1977–1978) and Seventh Edition (1979–1980), affirming her status as a documented political figure.

Together, Claude and Ruth raised two daughters, Vanessa and Mary Broussard, who continued the family's presence in Arcola. The Broussard household also included Claude Jr.'s siblings, Doris, Floyd, William T. H., Raymond, Rosemary, and Tommy, forming a large, stable family structure typical of rural Black communities in the mid-twentieth century.

The Broussards maintained their own burial ground, the Claude J. Broussard Family Cemetery, located on land once owned by the family. This cemetery, formally recognized by Fort Bend County as Cemetery FB-C046, stands as a testament to the family's rooted presence and the stewardship of their own history. Claude Jr. is buried there, and the site remains a physical marker of the family's legacy in Arcola.

Their presence is also marked in the landscape itself: Broussard Lane, a county-recognized roadway in Arcola, bears the family name and stands as a visible reminder of their long-standing roots in the community.

The Broussards' legacy lives on through their family cemetery, their civic service, their land, and the memories preserved by those who knew them. In restoring their story, the Broussards take their rightful place among the families who sustained Arcola across generations.

Leavings Concrete Company

Leavings Concrete Company, located at 2203 McKeever Road near Arcola, Texas, has operated continuously since 1969, making it one of the longest-running rural concrete contractors in northern Brazoria and southern Fort Bend counties. The business was founded and operated by Donald R. "Don" Leavings, a white tradesman whose small, family-run crew became a familiar presence in the region's agricultural and residential construction landscape.

With a workforce of two to four employees and an annual revenue between $100,000 and $500,000, Leavings Concrete functioned as a classic rural contractor — steady, local, and deeply embedded in the community's labor economy. The company specialized in driveways, patios, foundations, stamped concrete, and general concrete work, serving both residential and small commercial clients across Arcola, Rosharon, Fresno, and the surrounding farm-to-market corridors.

Like many white contractors of the mid- to late-twentieth century, Don Leavings relied on a mixed workforce that included skilled Black laborers from Arcola's long-standing families. Men from the Hall family, in particular, were frequently hired for forming, pouring, and finishing work — a labor relationship remembered across generations in Arcola's oral history. These crews formed the backbone of rural construction, shaping the driveways, slabs, porches, and small foundations that defined the built environment of the region.

In community memory, the company's name was often pronounced as "Leving," reflecting the way contractor names were transmitted orally rather than through written records.

Despite this phonetic shift, Leavings Concrete maintained a strong reputation for reliability and craftsmanship, remaining active for more than five decades and contributing significantly to the physical and economic landscape of Arcola and its neighboring communities.

From a Seed to a Cornerstone

The Story of Community Express Inc.

Founded in 1996, Community Express Inc. has been a cornerstone of support for low- to moderate-income families in Arcola and Fresno, Fort Bend County, Texas. The seed was planted two years earlier, in 1994, when Congresswoman Sheila Jackson Lee, speaking at a Juvenile Justice Conference in Austin, declared: *Too often when people need us the most, we give them our worst.* Hearing those words, Priscilla T. Graham was moved to embrace servant leadership. Together with Veeda V. Williams, she transformed that inspiration into action, creating Community Express Inc. to serve the community in a greater capacity.

For over 30 years, the organization has provided educational and charitable assistance through impactful programs. Its flagship STEMulating SUCCESS Project motivates youth through personal development, academic enrichment, civic awareness, and stress-management tools. Family enrichment programs further strengthen households, tailored to the unique needs of the community.

Over the decades, Community Express Inc. has expanded its reach through partnerships with Fort Bend County, The George Foundation, Fort Bend Parks and Recreation, H-E-B, and the City of Arcola. These collaborations have sustained and grown its programs, ensuring families continue to benefit from a wide range of opportunities.

With more than 30 years of continuous service, Community Express Inc. remains a trusted institution, striving to uplift and empower families through education and enrichment. What began with a single quote in 1994 grew into an enduring organization, proving that words of truth, when acted upon, can transform generations.

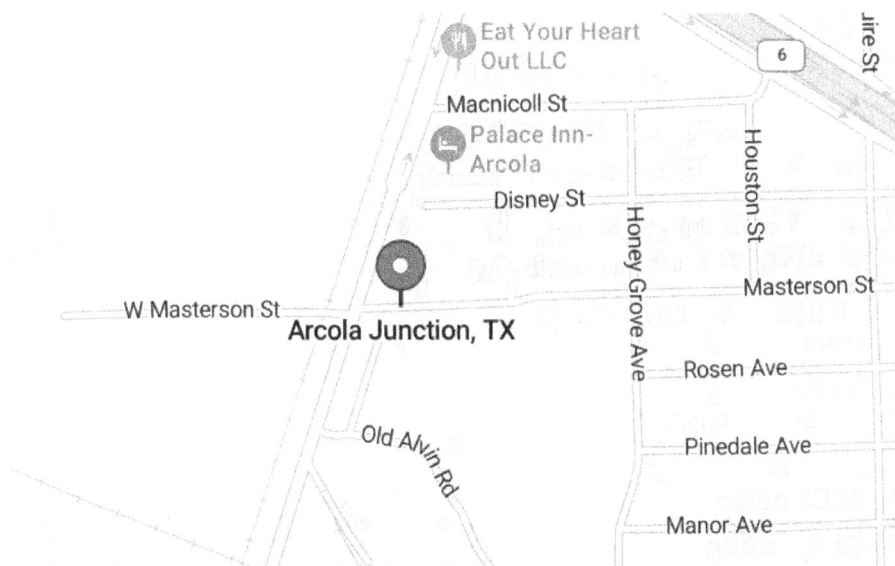

Arcola Two Junctions

Arcola has two junctions, but only one holds its soul. While today's developers and maps often mark Highway 6 and FM 521 as the town's commercial *gateway*, that designation is recent and transactional. The true heart of Arcola lies farther south at FM 521 and Masterson Street, the sacred crossroads where railroads did not just connect stations, they stitched together Black futures. Here, formerly enslaved people, postwar settlers, and generational families claimed space on land grounded in Abstracts 25, 31, 170, and 352, historic surveys that became living testimony.

This junction, nestled within these foundational land grants, was never just about tracks; it was about transformation. Along iron rails laid in 1858 by the Houston Tap and Brazoria Railway, Black mobility gained direction. When the Arcola Post Office was established at this site in 1869, it did more than deliver mail; it formally conferred the name Arcola, legitimizing a thriving community built on labor, land, and faith. Federal maps, railroad schedules, and county records finally mirrored what the people had already made real.

Even before Arcola's designation as a railroad junction in 1878, this land had already been spiritually claimed. Families rooted their futures not in infrastructure, but in memory, resilience, and sacred geography. The junction emerged as a nucleus, woven into the very fabric of the land itself: Abstracts 25, 31, 170, and 352, all part of Arcola's early geography of resistance, where civic life was seeded and sustained.

Palestine Missionary Baptist Church

During slavery, slaves developed strong religious convictions and the desire to control their own church services. However, in many cases slave owners refused to allow them to conduct services without Anglo supervision. Some owners allowed their slaves to attend segregated services and permitted Black preachers to reside over the rural gathering, or they paid Anglo circuit riders to deliver periodic sermons to the slave congregation. Occasionally, slave congregations were allowed to join white religious associations. To keep control of their religious beliefs, slaves often slipped away into the woods to hold their own services free from Anglo influence.

After the Civil War, Emancipation provided Freedmen with the opportunity to move away from prejudice and establish their own congregations and churches, with many becoming either Baptists or Methodists. The Palestine Missionary Baptist Church at Daniels Road 7414, Arcola, Texas, was founded in 1870 at the original site of Arcola in the William Hall Survey.

The Railroad Bed at Hawdon

Subsequently, the congregation relocated to the edge of the Arcola
Plantation, near a railroad switch called Hawdon.

New St. Philip Missionary Baptist Church

The New St. Philip Missionary Baptist Church, located at 6135
Highway 521, was established in 1923 following a split from Saint
Phillips Baptist Church. Initially, services were held under a brush
arbor. Reverend Johnnie J. Bullock was chosen as the first pastor,
alongside four officers: Deacon Collie Sessum, Deacon Ed Tripple,

Sister Shelia Britton, and Brother Allen Posley. The founding members included Brother Jim Dade, Sister Mary Dade, Sister Minnie Bullock, Sister Virginia Rodgers, Sister Jessie Williams, Sister Lucy Davis, and Sister Ollie Sessum. Later, services moved to a tent in the Mulberry area near DeWalt, Texas, and the church's name was changed to New Saint Philip. During this time, Reverend Thomas Robinson served as pastor.

Brother Jimmie Dade, a dedicated congregation member, approached his employer, Mr. A. L. Choen, a realtor, to request land for the church. Mr. Choen generously agreed to donate the land on which the church currently stands. Reverend J. J. Bullock oversaw the construction of the first church building. After his resignation, Reverend Houston served as pastor but resigned twice. Eventually, Reverend C. H. Jones took over the leadership. Reverend R. E. Edward was then called to lead the church, serving for eight years, followed by Reverend D. A. Goston, who served for eleven years before resigning. The contributions and indomitable spirit of these leaders, who tirelessly served the church, will never be forgotten.

Reverend J. N. Williams was later called to lead New St. Philip Baptist Church. He made significant contributions to the church and the surrounding community with a forward-thinking approach. Pastor Williams, who came from Houston, Texas, faced considerable opposition; however, with the strength of God and His Spirit, he seized every opportunity to serve as pastor. Under his leadership, the church made remarkable progress in the ministry and improved its facilities. After 33 years of dedicated service, the Lord called Pastor Williams home in February 1998.

On April 13, 1998, the church elected Reverend J. DeWitt Clark as the new pastor. A visionary young man, Pastor Clark revitalized the church and oversaw growth in membership and understanding of the Word of God. He also restored the original spelling of the church's name to New St. Philip Missionary Baptist Church. Pastor Clark has introduced various ministries throughout his tenure to enhance discipleship and strengthen connections with the local community.

Daniel Perry Historical Marker

This marker commemorates Daniel Perry, one of the early settlers who arrived in Texas in 1832. He was born in 1791 in Mississippi. In 1832, Perry moved to Texas with his wife, Eliza Whitehead, and their two sons. After Eliza's death, he married Louisa Ann Morton in 1833. Together, they had four children and lived on land Louisa inherited from the David Fitzgerald League. Perry joined the Texas Army as a captain and recruiter, participating in the Battle of San Jacinto and serving in the Republic of Texas Navy. In 1837, he signed the petition to establish Fort Bend County. After losing Louisa, he remarried Jane Hamblen in 1851.

Duke Community Historical Marker

This marker highlights the contributions of early settlers, including David Fitzgerald, Thomas Barnett, and Moses Shipman. In 1824, the Old Three Hundred settlers David Fitzgerald, Thomas Barnett, and Moses Shipman were granted land in this area. Fitzgerald fought at Anahuac in 1832, while Barnett signed the Texas Declaration of Independence. The location on a high northeastern bluff overlooking Clear Lake provided an ample water supply for steam engines,

facilitating railroad construction in the mid-1800s. Duke served as the terminus of the Sugar Land Railway, primarily used for transporting sugarcane. The area developed into a central shipping point featuring a store, a hotel, a livestock pen, and sugar mills. It was named after Duke Hessey, the storekeeper. The village had a post office from 1883 to 1922, with J.R. Fenn as its first postmaster. Today, the only remnant of this once-thriving community is the Duke Cemetery. The Houston Southwest Airport spans 165 acres, while CEMEX occupies 219.5 acres of land that was once part of Duke. Both properties are located within the City of Arcola.

The Fitzgerald and Fenn Families Historical Marker

This marker honors David Fitzgerald, a veteran of the American Revolution and the War of 1812, and his son-in-law, Eli Fenn. Fitzgerald moved from Georgia to Texas in 1821, followed by Fenn in 1832. Fenn participated in the Texas Revolution and signed the petition to establish Fort Bend County in 1837. His wife, Sarah, was skilled in natural remedies and vital in caring for the sick in their community.

Eli Fenn's son, John Rutherford Fenn, was a Confederate Army veteran. He was also the first postmaster of Duke and one of the first officers chosen for the Jay-bird Democratic Association of Fort Bend County, organized in 1889. He served on the Executive Committee, and his eldest son, F.M.O. (Otis) Fenn, was the secretary.

F.M.O. Fenn served as County Attorney and later became Justice of Peace. In 1893, the Sons of the Republic of Texas were organized in his office in Richmond. Rebecca Williams, John Rutherford Fenn's wife, was a charter member of the Daughters of the Republic of Texas. Sarah, John Rutherford, and Rebecca Fenn are buried in Duke Cemetery.

In 1981, Laura Dietz Fenn, the widow of Joseph Johnson Fenn Jr. (Mr. Button), sold the last piece of land belonging to David Fitzgerald's descendants for development. This land was transformed into the One Oak Chase Subdivision on Fenn Road in Arcola.

A Rural Legacy in Arcola's Layered Geography

Built in 1928, this modest residence stands on 1.6 acres carved from the David Fitzgerald Survey, Abstract 25. Modest in scale at 1,400 square feet with three bedrooms and two baths, its nearly century-long presence makes it one of the oldest surviving homes in Arcola. Unlike the civic institutions clustered in the Thomas Hall survey, this property reflects the rural homestead tradition where families established farms and households in the early twentieth century. Its endurance offers a rare architectural and genealogical link to Arcola's formative years, situating it within the broader story of land grants, subdivision, and community building in Fort Bend County.

Just north of the Fitzgerald tract where the 1928 home stands, Arcola School Road anchors the Thomas Hall survey and the institutions that defined Arcola's civic life. By the early 1900s, Freedmen families had established schools, churches, and cemeteries along this corridor, creating a community core distinct from the surrounding farmsteads. The proximity of this homestead to Arcola School Road illustrates the layered geography of Arcola, with households rooted in land grants and communal institutions rooted in Hall's survey. Together, they reveal how Arcola's residents built both private dwellings and shared spaces of education, worship, and remembrance, weaving a durable fabric of community across survey lines.

The McKeever Road Cottage

The McKeever Road Cottage stands as a modest one-bedroom home, a rare witness to Arcola's mid-twentieth-century rural expansion. Built in 1948 on 1.51 acres within the Manuel Escalero Survey, Abstract 170, the dwelling measures just over 700 square feet. Its wood-frame simplicity and composition shingle roof reflect the working-family roots of the area. The parcel's legal description anchors it in Texas's nineteenth-century land grant system, embedding the property within Fort Bend County's settlement history.

McKeever Road itself has long served as a vital artery through Arcola, linking residents to Highway 6 and framing decades of civic debate over land use, infrastructure, and community agency. In the early 2000s, proposals to realign the road for airport expansion sparked controversy, as residents feared condemnation and displacement. Situated at the heart of these debates, the house embodies both continuity and resistance against external pressures.

As one of the few surviving mid-century rural dwellings in Arcola, the property offers a tangible link to the post-war settlement patterns that shaped the town. Its endurance across generations restores dignity to households often absent from the documentary record, funeral programs, obituaries, and small business archives that rarely survive. The Escalero Survey lineage connects the parcel to the earliest land grants, while the house itself reflects the persistence of families who carved homes from grant land and maintained agency in the face of county development. Today, more than a small rural cottage, the property, purchased by Francisco and Carmen Roque in 1998, stands as a living artifact of Arcola's transition from land grant survey to modern community.

Its presence offers descendants and historians a window into the lived experience of Arcola's early modern era, embodying both the persistence of its families and the pressures that have defined the town's identity. In the front and back yards, aluminum disks set by the U.S. Coast & Geodetic Survey in 1952 anchor the site to the nation's geodetic network. Embedded in concrete and stamped as reference marks, they testify to the moment when Arcola's rural landscape was drawn into the federal grid of surveying and floodplain planning, linking a modest cottage to the broader story of land, agency, and continuity.

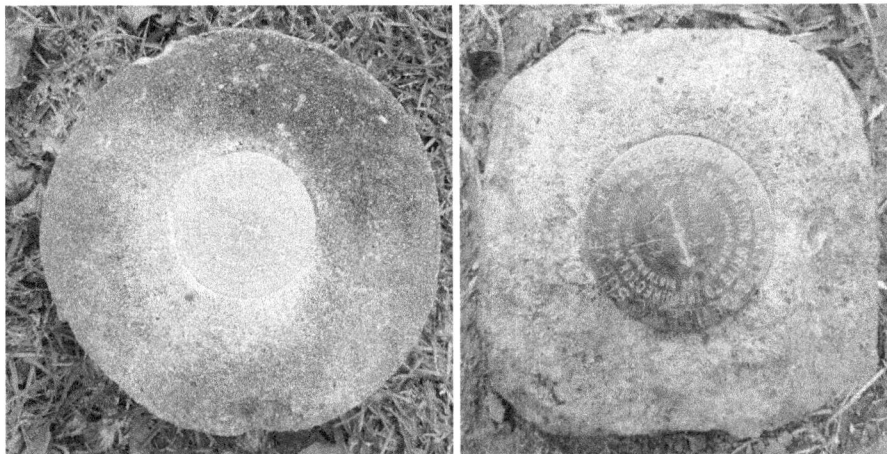

These marks tie a single Arcola homestead into the national geodetic framework of the United States, underscoring their significance. When the U.S. Coast & Geodetic Survey set them in 1952, they established permanent control points enabling engineers, mapmakers, and governments to measure land, water, and infrastructure with precision.

For Arcola, this meant the property became part of the official backbone of American mapping and floodplain planning. The marks helped define elevations for drainage projects, supported highway and airport surveys, and ensured that deeds and boundaries could be measured against a federally recognized standard. In a community where oral testimony and family landholding often outweigh formal documentation, the presence of federal survey plates is rare and powerful: they provide irrefutable evidence of place, continuity, and national recognition. From a historical perspective, they show that even a modest rural cottage was drawn into the larger story of land control and infrastructure development, transforming the house from a local landmark into a recognized point of reference in the nation's mapping history.

L. M. INKLEY COMPANY

OWNERS and DEVELOPERS

Main Offices 4337 Liberty Road

HOUSTON, TEXAS

Nite Headquarters:
6919 STAFFORDSHIRE BLVD.
JAckson 8-6745

Telephone:
OR 3-5621
OR 3-6747

Date___FEBRUARY 9TH, 1957___

We agree to build for:___JAMES WILLIAMS AND WIFE, ~~PHIXXXXE~~ PHILLIPPE ~~XXXXXXXX~~ WILLIAMS,___

Address___ROUTE #1m BOX 127, ROSHARON, TEXAS.___ Telephone___

A 4 Room House, plus hall and bath and 6'X8' porch, all finished on outside and semi-finished on inside, as per sample shown, wired for lights, piped for gas inside house, pitcher pump well in yard and outhouse built with water tig box. House painted two coats best white paint on outside, screens on windows and doors. Roof to be___GREEN___in color and trim on the house to match.

Price of above house as sample shown is $ 3,760.00

_____plus 8% interest.

Your ~~LOXXX~~ WEST HALF LOT ~~XX~~ #27,_____Block #___1___
(52 1/5 FT X 600 FEET DEEP) ON GRAVEL STREET.

In Addition___ARCOLA FARMS___
Fort Bend
~~Harris~~ County, Texas to be your down payment.

$ 40.00
House to be completed by___MARCH 20TH, 1957___,First payment of $~~35.00~~
FORTY
(~~Thirty-Five~~ Dollars) including 8% interest to become due_APRIL 20TH, 1957_

and on the_20TH_day of each month thereafter until the full amount of

$___3,760.00_____plus 8% interest has been paid.

Above price includes cost of Mortgage Title Policy, drawing of papers, filing of papers and first year's insurance. HOME ON OUTSIDE AND INSIDE LIKE OUR SAMPLE HOME #1 ON OUR OFFICE GROUNDS AT 4339 LIBERTY ROAD, "THE TRUMMIE CAIN SPECIAL, WITH EXCEPTION OF ON INSIDE, ALL TRIMMED OUT, WITH KITCHEN CABINETS & WOODEN DRAIN BOARD IN KITCHEN. ALL WALLS FLOATED & TAPED, READY T PAINT BUT NOT PAINTED. OUTSIDE TO HAVE 105 SIDING INSTEAD OF BEADED SIDING PORCH SIDE OF THE FRONT. ONE DOOR ON INSIDE BETWEEN LIVING ROOM & HALL.

Signed:

ACKNOWLEDGED:

James Williams

Phillippe Williams

L.M. INKLEY COMPANY

BY:_____

BLOSSOM HEIGHTS

Benny Brown Addition - Washington Addition - Ballard Gardens - Sheffield Gardens - Liberty Garden Tracts - Victory Garden Tracts

Fair Grounds Park Annex Addition - Chew Addition - Liberty Addition - Blueberry Terrace - Colonia De Juarez

Rest Lawn Cemetery, Inc. - Liberty Road Manor - Liberty Terrace - Dreamland Place - McNair Heights

222

The Trummie Cain Special

L.M. Inkley Company, headquartered at 4337 Liberty Road in Houston with a secondary office on Staffordshire Boulevard, was a mid-twentieth-century developer that openly marketed *Properties Exclusively for Colored People.* Through extensive advertising campaigns in Houston newspapers, the company promoted what it called *12 Additions for Colored People*, a network of segregated subdivisions designed for Black American families excluded from mainstream housing markets. These additions included Blossom Heights, Benny Brown Addition, Washington Addition, Ballard Gardens, Sheffield Gardens, Liberty Garden Tracts, Navy Garden Tracts, Fair Grounds Park Annex Addition, Chew Addition, Liberty Addition, Blueberry Terrace, Colonia De Juarez, Rest Lawn Cemetery, Liberty Road Manor, Liberty Terrace, Dreamland Place, and McNair Heights. Each was marketed with installment terms that mirrored rent payments, creating a pathway to land ownership while reinforcing racial boundaries in housing.

In Fort Bend County, Inkley extended its reach to Arcola. A surviving 1957 agreement between L.M. Inkley Company and James and Philippe Williams documents the construction of their home on the west half of Lot 27, Block 1 in Arcola Farms. The contract specified the construction of a four-room house with a hall, bath, porch, and basic utilities, priced at $3,760 plus 8% interest, with monthly payments of $40. The buyers' lot served as the down payment, and the agreement included the title policy, filing fees, and insurance. The house model was branded as *The Trummie Cain Special*, referencing Houston radio promoter Trummie Cain, whose broadcasts and talent shows were central to Black cultural life in the 1940s and 1950s.

Cain's nightly program on KATL radio was marketed as reaching Houston's *forgotten 200,000* Black listeners, and his Lincoln Theater talent contests launched the careers of local musicians such as Weldon *Juke Boy* Bonner. By attaching Cain's name to a home model, Inkley leveraged his popularity and credibility, aligning its segregated housing product with a figure who symbolized Black achievement and visibility.

The Arcola Farms contract illustrates Inkley's broader business model: installment contracts, low down payments, and racially exclusive marketing. It situates Arcola within the larger geography of segregated development that stretched from Houston's Liberty Road corridor to rural tracts in Fort Bend County. Advertisements confirm that Inkley marketed similar properties in Houston's east and south sides, near Sunnyside and Chocolate Bayou, and extended promotions to other Texas locales such as Liberty and Moscow in Polk County. Together, these developments formed a network of segregated subdivisions that offered Black American families access to land and housing, but only within racially bounded spaces. The legacy of these additions is twofold: they provided opportunities for ownership and community building, while simultaneously entrenching segregation and limiting access to mainstream financing and neighborhoods.

Echoes of Mid-Century Arcola

This modest, single-story dwelling was built in the city of Arcola. It features light siding, simple rectangular massing, and a partially framed porch that lacks ornamentation. Its proportions, window placement, and utilitarian construction resemble rural vernacular homes built in Texas during the mid-20th century, particularly between the 1940s and 1960s. The weathered exterior and skeletal porch framing reinforce this impression, standing in contrast to the more standardized layouts and materials typical of 1990s construction. County appraisal records list the house as built in 1994, but this date may reflect a later remodel, the point at which the structure was added to the tax rolls, or a default entry when earlier documentation was missing. Such discrepancies are common in rural communities where official records often lag behind lived reality, leaving buildings that visually and materially belong to an earlier era misclassified in modern databases.

Resource-Driven Building Practices

The house was built in 1925 and is located in Abstract 25, David Fitzgerald Survey. Its architectural features reflect vernacular rural construction typical of Texas during that era. Wooden plank siding with horizontal boards, a simple gable roof originally covered with corrugated metal or wood shingles, and construction on short piers or a shallow foundation are all consistent with homes built in this period. The absence of decorative trim or ornamentation further underscores a utilitarian design, shaped by the straightforward, resource-driven building practices common in rural communities of the time.

Resource-driven building practices in rural Texas during the early to mid-20th century produced homes that were simple, functional, and constructed with materials readily at hand. Timber from local mills was commonly used for plank siding, while corrugated metal or wood shingles provided affordable roofing. Foundations were often shallow or raised on short piers, a practical solution for flood-prone ground that required fewer resources than poured concrete. Ornamentation was rare, as decorative trim or elaborate porches demanded skilled labor and additional expense that most families could not justify. These houses embodied a utilitarian approach, built by hand or with community labor, emphasizing durability and necessity over aesthetics. This reliance on local materials and shared effort defined the vernacular character of rural homes from the 1920s through the 1950s.

The house located in the Arcola Farms Subdivision stands as a remarkable example of vernacular architecture from the early to mid-twentieth century. Its corrugated metal roof, wooden lap siding, and straightforward rectangular form with a front porch reflect the practical construction methods of the period, when families relied on locally available materials and hand labor rather than formal architectural plans. These features speak to the resilience and resourcefulness of Freedmen-descendant families who established homesteads in Arcola during the decades following emancipation. The structure's weathered surfaces and adaptive additions, such as porch railings and ramps, are not simply signs of age but evidence of endurance, showing how the house has persisted across generations while remaining part of a living landscape.

Although the exact year of construction is undocumented, the architectural evidence situates the house between the 1920s and 1950s. This dating range means that the structure is already between seventy and one hundred years old, and if its origins lie in the 1920s or early 1930s, it has already crossed the century mark. The possibility of being over one hundred years old elevates the house into the category of century candidate structures. Its longevity underscores the durability of materials such as old-growth lumber and corrugated metal, which were chosen for their availability and strength, and it highlights the remarkable endurance of vernacular craftsmanship in Arcola.

When compared to modern houses, the longevity of this structure becomes even more striking. Early homes like this one were built with dense, slow-grown timber that resisted rot and insects, whereas modern houses rely on faster-grown, softer lumber that is less durable. The craftsmanship of the early twentieth century emphasized permanence, with homes often built by families themselves, whereas contemporary construction prioritizes speed and cost efficiency.

Traditional materials such as wood, brick, stone, and copper were selected for their proven ability to last decades, even centuries, while modern homes increasingly use plastics, composites, and engineered wood that are efficient but not always as enduring. As a result, many vernacular homes from the 1920s to 1950s remain standing after nearly a century, while modern houses are often designed for lifespans of fifty to seventy years before requiring major renovation or replacement.

The cultural significance of the Arcola Farms house lies not only in its physical endurance but in its role as a living artifact of community identity. It represents the resilience of families who built and sustained homes despite systemic barriers, the continuity of generations who adapted and maintained the structure, and the tangible imprint of everyday lives that shaped Arcola's history. As part of the Arcola Farms Subdivision, this house connects past and present, standing as a heritage marker that embodies dignity, survival, and continuity. For archival purposes, it should be indexed within Abstract 25 with subdivision reference, surname linkage, and citation placeholders to ensure clarity and accountability. Its potential century-long endurance makes it a cornerstone of Arcola's living heritage and a powerful reminder of the architectural and cultural legacy of Freedmen-descendant communities.

Fenn Road

Fenn Road takes its name from the Fenn family, one of the early landholding families in the Arcola area. More than a simple thoroughfare, the road serves as a physical marker of history, tracing the boundary line between the Thomas Barnett and David Fitzgerald surveys. Both surveys were part of Stephen F. Austin's Old Three Hundred land grants of 1824, which laid the foundation for settlement in Fort Bend County. The placement of Fenn Road along this dividing line reflects how survey boundaries shaped the geography of Arcola, determining not only property lines but also the routes by which families traveled, farmed, and connected their households to neighboring communities. In this way, Fenn Road embodies both family legacy and the larger story of Texas's earliest Anglo-American colonization, anchoring Arcola's modern landscape in the land grant system that defined the region nearly two centuries ago.

McKeever Road

McKeever Road is a historically significant east–west corridor in Arcola, originally cut through the Manuel Escalero Survey, Abstract 170. It has long served as a critical connector between rural homesteads and Highway 6, facilitating local travel and commerce. The road features mid-twentieth-century dwellings, including a notable 1948 one-bedroom home at the McKeever Road Cottage, exemplifying rural expansion during that period.

Named after the McKeever family, whose extensive landholdings anchored the corridor, McKeever Road reflects the influence of prominent local families on settlement and development patterns in Fort Bend County. While the exact year the road was named is not definitively documented, the McKeever name has been associated with the area since at least the mid-1900s.

In recent years, McKeever Road has experienced increased attention due to its proximity to Houston Southwest Airport and ongoing commercial development. The area around the road includes private gated properties, office and storage buildings, and small businesses such as Bean Here Coffee Labs and Tycalk 9, reflecting a shift from purely rural to mixed-use commercial and residential activity.

As of the mid-2020s, Fort Bend County and the city of Arcola have collaborated on infrastructure improvements, including plans to rebuild and enhance McKeever Road to accommodate growing traffic and development pressures. This ongoing investment underscores the road's continued importance as a vital artery within the community.

McKeever Road remains a living artifact of Arcola's evolution, preserving the legacy of early land grant surveys and family influence while adapting to modern growth and economic change.

Thomas Lane Taylor

Thomas Lane Taylor was a pioneering civic leader whose election as county commissioner during Reconstruction marked a turning point in Fort Bend County politics. In a period when Black residents outnumbered whites nearly three to one, Taylor rose to office alongside figures like District Clerk C.M. Ferguson and Sheriff Walter Moses Burton, later a Texas senator and co-founder of Prairie View A&M University. Their victories opened a brief but remarkable era of representative democracy in post–Civil War Texas.

Taylor's service ended abruptly in 1888, when the Jaybird–Woodpecker feud forced Black officials from power under threat of violence. Ordered to leave within ten hours, he relocated his family from Kendleton to Boone's Bend in Wharton County.

Though exiled, Taylor's legacy endured. In 2015, Missouri City named Thomas Taylor Parkway in his honor, restoring his place to civic memory.

Arcola Community Cemetery

Arcola Community Cemetery, cataloged as FB-C057 by the Fort Bend County Historical Commission, is a small, endangered burial ground tied to Arcola Plantation. Located at coordinates 29.477744, -95.483861, the cemetery covers about 1.75 acres of private land and requires permission for access. Historic records place it along *Scanlan Road*, with *Scanlan Parkway* running nearby; both thoroughfares exist today, reflecting the layered development of the plantation corridor. Though neglected and vulnerable to development pressures, the cemetery remains a vital landmark, anchoring descendants and researchers to the lived reality of Arcola Plantation and preserving a rare physical link to families whose presence might otherwise be obscured.

Burnside Cemetery

Burnside Cemetery, cataloged as FB-C158 by the Fort Bend County Historical Commission, is an inactive burial ground tied to Arcola Plantation. Also known historically as *Fenn Plantation Cemetery*, it is located off Federal Way in Sugar Land, Texas, at coordinates 29.50370, -95.50101. The cemetery covers about 0.25 acres and has been disturbed by developers, with graves now located under a park, street, and some houses. Its placement near the old plantation corridor situates it within the broader agricultural and transportation landscape that sustained Arcola's operations. Though neglected and fragile in condition, Burnside Cemetery remains a vital landmark, preserving the connection between the Fenn family's tenure on Arcola Plantation and the community histories embedded in its land. More than its visible remains, the cemetery endures as a witness to Fort Bend County's plantation past, offering descendants and researchers a rare physical link to lives and stories that might otherwise be obscured.

House Cemetery

House Cemetery, cataloged as FB-C150 by the Fort Bend County Historical Commission, is an inactive burial ground tied to Arcola Plantation. Located off McKeever Road in Sugar Land, Texas, at coordinates 29.49967, -95.51689, the cemetery lies on private property and requires permission for access. Historic surveys note its placement along the railroad corridor that once served the plantation, situating it within the broader transportation network that carried sugar and other crops from Arcola. Though neglected and fragile in condition, the cemetery remains a vital landmark, preserving the connection between the House family's tenure on Arcola Plantation and the community histories embedded in its land. More than its visible remains, House Cemetery endures as a witness to Fort Bend County's plantation past, offering descendants and researchers a rare physical link to lives and stories that might otherwise be obscured.

Waters Cemetery

Waters Cemetery, cataloged as FB-C128 by the Fort Bend County Historical Commission, is an inactive burial ground tied to Arcola Plantation. Located on present-day Sienna Plantation in Sugar Land, Texas, at coordinates 29.49814, -95.55229, the cemetery lies on private property and requires permission for access. Historic surveys place it near the railroad corridor and levee system along the Brazos River, situating it within the plantation's transportation and agricultural landscape. Though neglected and fragile in condition, the cemetery remains a vital landmark, preserving the connection between the Waters family's tenure on Arcola Plantation and the community histories embedded in its land. More than its visible remains, Waters Cemetery endures as a witness to Fort Bend County's plantation past, offering descendants and researchers a rare physical link to lives and stories that might otherwise be obscured.

Harris Family Cemetery

Harris Family Cemetery was established in 1890 and is located near Long Point Creek and Fort Bend Toll Road, Arcola. It contains the graves of Lola V. Harris, Albert L. Harris and serves as a resting place for members of the Harris family and other community members.

Juliff Area Cemetery

Juliff Area Cemetery, also known as Mount Tabor Baptist Church Cemetery or Mount Tabor Cemetery, is located at 211 Porter Road. The oldest known grave is Sandy Colbert, who was born in 1878 and passed away on August 8, 1916. The size of the cemetery is 0.27 acres.

The Riceton-Arcola Cemetery

The Riceton-Arcola Cemetery, also known as the Arcola-Fresno Cemetery, is located in Fresno, Fort Bend County, Texas, near the intersection of Rabb/Burford Road (FM 521) and Sycamore. The earliest documented burial dates to July 4, 1853. The cemetery encompasses approximately 1.54 acres, according to county survey records. The inclusion of Arcola in the name reflects historic ties to the neighboring community, whose families shared the burial ground with those of Fresno in the late 19th and early 20th centuries. The Riceton-Arcola or Arcola-Fresno designation underscores this dual identity: Riceton was a nearby farming area, Fresno was the geographic location, and Arcola was the closest incorporated town with social and institutional connections to the families interred there. Although the cemetery lies outside Arcola's city limits and ETJ, the name preserves the community's role in its establishment and maintenance. This dual naming is consistent with conventions in Fort Bend County, where cemeteries often carry the names of multiple neighboring communities to reflect the breadth of families they served.

Mount Pilgrim Baptist Church Cemetery

The Mount Pilgrim Baptist Church Cemetery, also known in some records as Mount Tabor Cemetery, is located in Arcola, Texas, directly across from 9615 FM 521. Though the original church structure no longer stands, the cemetery remains a vital landmark of Black religious and civic life in the region. It holds the names of families who anchored Arcola's community through faith, education, and land stewardship, including members of the Hayes, Sessums, Cobb, and Delaney lineages. Modest in size but rich in historical weight, the 0.27-acre site preserves memory where formal records are sparse, offering a quiet but powerful testament to the lives lived and legacies left behind.

Duke Cemetery

Duke Cemetery is located across Clear Lake, southwest of Duke, and contains the graves of Sarah Fitzgerald Fenn, John Rutherford Fenn, Rebecca Williams Fenn, members of the Williams family, Daniel Perry, Perry children, and Mrs. Hubbard. Probably Louisa Ann Morton Perry and her mother, Nancy Spencer Morton, are also buried in this area, as well as David Fitzgerald. In 1901, W. P. Hamblin, son of Jane Hogue Hamblin Perry, wife of Daniel Perry, deeded a part of the old Perry homestead to be set aside as a cemetery. There are no headstones in Duke Cemetery.

Lawson Family Cemetery

Lawson Family Cemetery is located near Scanlan Road, Arcola. The earliest burial is 1953.

McKeever Cemetery

McKeever Cemetery is located on Lawson Road, Arcola. The earliest burial was on November 30, 1980.

Shipman League Cemetery

Shipman League Cemetery is located near Knight Road, Arcola. Moses Guy Shipman, born in 1816 and died in 1836, is the oldest known burial in this family cemetery, containing seven other members of the Shipman family.

From Convict Leasing to Museum Memory

The land that became the Central State Farm in Sugar Land, Texas, began as a sugar plantation in 1878 under the convict leasing system. Freedmen and other Black men were disproportionately targeted by discriminatory laws such as vagrancy statutes, then leased to private planters. Conditions were brutal, and prisoners were worked to death in cane fields, a reality confirmed by the 2018 discovery of the *Sugar Land 95* cemetery. This system was a continuation of slavery by another name, sustaining the sugar economy of Fort Bend County.

As the plantation changed hands, Imperial Sugar purchased it in 1907, and the following year, the State of Texas acquired the property. By 1909, it had become one of the first state-owned penal institutions.

Racial segregation defined the prison system, and Black prisoners were concentrated at Sugar Land, assigned to the hardest agricultural labor, such as cutting cane, clearing land, and maintaining ditches.

White prisoners were housed elsewhere or given less grueling assignments. Oral histories and archival research confirm that Central State Farm functioned as a *Black prison* during its formative decades, and it was Reginald Moore, community activist, historian, and founder of the Texas Slave Descendants Society, who insisted that this truth be documented and remembered. His advocacy, oral history interviews, and tireless campaigns for memorialization ensured that the racial exclusivity of the prison was not erased from public memory.

In 1932, the state constructed the Central State Farm main building to modernize administration and inmate housing. Designed by the Austin firm Gieseke and Harris, with consultation from F.E. Gieseke, professor of architecture, the structure was built of poured, reinforced concrete, a modern technique at the time. Its Art Moderne style featured stepped pilasters, chamfered corners, metal casement windows, and a square tower capped with a pyramidal roof. This was the first modernized prison building in Texas, symbolizing reforms in inmate classification and administration, though racial segregation persisted.

Despite the architectural reforms, the lived reality for Black prisoners remained harsh and unequal. They endured grueling agricultural labor that sustained the sugar industry, reinforcing the racialized exploitation that defined Texas's penal farms. The building itself embodied the state's attempt to bureaucratize and sanitize a system rooted in racial oppression, while the men inside continued to suffer under its weight. Moore's work made clear that this was not simply a prison, it was a labor camp designed to exploit Black bodies for economic gain, and his insistence on tying the Central Unit's legacy to the broader story of convict leasing reframed how the community understood its past.

For decades, the Central Unit, which included the Central State Farm building, operated as one of Texas's major prison farms, housing up to 950 men. In 2011, it became the first Texas prison to shut down without replacement. During the redevelopment of the land into the Telfair master-planned community, the main building was preserved for its historical importance.

Today, that preserved structure houses the Fort Bend Museum, anchoring local history and reminding visitors of Sugar Land's dual legacy of sugar and prisons. Its survival ensures that the community can confront the legacy of convict leasing, segregation, and forced labor that shaped Fort Bend County. As a museum, the building now serves as a site of reflection, offering a space to understand the intertwined heritage of sugar production, incarceration, and Black labor in Texas.

And thanks to Reginald Moore's relentless advocacy, the story of the Central State Farm is not just about architecture or reform; it is about memory, justice, and the descendants whose lives were shaped by its shadow.

Reginald Moore

Reginald Moore was the steward of Sugar Land's buried history, a relentless activist whose vision transformed silence into remembrance. His life reflected a deep commitment to truth-telling and community memory. Born in Houston, he worked as a longshoreman and briefly as a prison guard at the Jester State Prison Farm in the 1980s. That experience haunted him: he witnessed Black inmates laboring under white overseers in conditions that echoed slavery. After retiring from the docks in the late 1990s, Moore dedicated himself full-time to researching the history of Texas prison farms and the brutal convict leasing system that sustained Sugar Land's sugar economy.

Moore founded the Texas Slave Descendants Society, through which he advocated for memorials, public recognition, and reparative justice for those who suffered under convict leasing. He repeatedly warned Fort Bend Independent School District and local officials that unmarked graves likely existed on former prison farmland. His warnings were ignored until 2018, when construction crews uncovered the remains of 95 Black prisoners, later named the Sugar

Land 95. This discovery vindicated Moore's decades of research and activism.

Despite resistance from city and county leaders, Moore persisted in demanding that the victims of convict leasing be honored. He partnered with Rice University's Woodson Research Center in 2015 to preserve his research archives, ensuring that scholars and descendants would have access to his work for generations. His efforts reframed Sugar Land's history, forcing acknowledgment that its prosperity was built on racialized forced labor.

Moore passed away on July 3, 2020, at the age of 60, from heart failure. He left behind a legacy as what colleagues called a *people's historian,* a man who carried the voices of the forgotten into public memory. His work ensured that the Central State Farm and the Sugar Land 95 would not be erased but instead recognized as central to Texas's story of incarceration, race, and labor.

Arcola Plantation on Oyster Creek
Antebellum Era

One of the most poignant remnants of the Arcola Plantation on Oyster Creek is the sugarhouse, also known as a sugar purgery. This building, where sugarcane was crushed, its juice extracted, and then boiled down to produce sugar, stands as a silent witness to the grueling labor that once took place within its walls.

Before the Civil War, the Arcola Plantation was one of the largest in Texas, thriving on the backbreaking work of enslaved people. The conditions were harsh, and the labor was relentless, making sugar cultivation one of the most brutal forms of agricultural work. The sugarhouse, with its weathered walls and echoes of the past, serves as a stark reminder of this painful history.

Other remnants of the Arcola Plantation include:

Sugar Bowls: Antebellum-era sugar factory large metal bowls used in the sugar production process during the antebellum era, now displayed in Heritage Park. These bowls, once filled with boiling sugar, now stand empty, symbolizing the end of an era marked by suffering and toil.

Brick Building: An abandoned brick building that once served as a sugar factory before the Civil War. Its crumbling facade and silent halls speak volumes about the lives that were spent and lost within.

Barn: A barn used for storing equipment and possibly housing animals, often referred to as a *sugar barn*. This structure, though simple, was integral to the plantation's operations and the daily lives of those who worked there.

These remnants are not just physical structures; they are powerful symbols of a history that must not be forgotten. They remind us of the resilience of those who endured unimaginable hardships and the importance of remembering and honoring their stories.

Oyster Creek

Oyster Creek, a 52-mile-long stream in Texas, flows southeast from Fort Bend County through Brazoria County to the Gulf of Mexico. With historical significance dating back to 1528, when Álvar Núñez Cabeza de Vaca was believed to have landed at its mouth, the creek's banks were once inhabited by the Karankawa Indians.

By the 1820s, the fertile soil along Oyster Creek attracted many of Stephen F. Austin's Old Three Hundred families, who established plantations and often used the creek to transport cotton and sugarcane. The state later acquired the area in the 1880s for prison farms, and by the 1950s, mining oyster shells from the creek became a local industry, with the shells used in road construction and manufacturing.

In the 1990s, water from the creek's upper reaches was pumped from the Brazos River for agricultural and industrial purposes. Surrounded by water-tolerant hardwoods, conifers, and prairie grasses, Oyster Creek flows through a mostly flat terrain characterized by expansive clays.

Brazos River

The connection between Arcola and the Brazos River is deeply rooted in the town's history and development. The river has been a vital resource for the community since its early days.

In the mid-19th century, Jonathan Dawson Waters established the Arcola Plantation along the Brazos River. The plantation thrived due to the fertile land and ample water supply provided by the river. The Arcola Plantation even had a wharf on the Brazos River, which was crucial in transporting goods. This wharf facilitated the movement of cotton and sugar to markets, utilizing the river's natural route for transportation. The presence of the wharf highlights the integral connection between the plantation and the Brazos River, further emphasizing the river's importance in Arcola's history.

As Arcola grew, the Brazos River continued to support its agricultural activities. The river's water was essential for irrigation, ensuring the success of crops and the sustainability of the community. The Houston Tap Railroad, built in 1858, further connected Arcola to other parts of Texas, enabling agricultural products to reach broader markets. The river's presence influenced the development of the railroad, as it provided a natural route for transportation.

In the post-Civil War era, the Brazos River remained an essential resource for the newly formed community of formerly enslaved people in Arcola. The river's water supported domestic needs and agriculture, contributing to the town's growth and stability. The river's resources supported the town's economy and infrastructure.

In modern times, the Brazos River plays a vital role in Arcola's development. The Brazos River Authority manages the water resources of the Brazos River basin, ensuring that Arcola has access to clean and reliable water. This supports the city's ongoing growth and sustainability, providing water for domestic use, agriculture, and industry.

Overall, the Brazos River has been a lifeline for Arcola, shaping its history and contributing to its development. The river's influence on agriculture, transportation, and water supply has been instrumental in the city's growth and continues to support its future.

Eleven-year-old Houston Atlee excels academically, earning straight A's, and is an avid basketball player at MacGregor Elementary School in Third Ward.

First White House of the Republic of Texas

The First White House of the Republic of Texas was located at the intersection of Main Street and Preston Street (now known as 405 Main Street). It served as the residence for President Sam Houston from November 1837 to December 1838 and President Mirabeau B. Lamar from December 1838 to October 1839. Although the original building no longer exists, the Scanlan Building was constructed on this site in 1909 by the Scanlan sisters in honor of their father, Thomas Howe Scanlan, who was the mayor of Houston in the 1870s. Designed by the esteemed architectural firm D.H. Burnham & Company of Chicago, the eleven-story office building was one of the first in Houston to utilize a fireproof steel skeleton.

Scanlan Fountain

Dating back to 1891, the Scanlan Fountain has a storied history and has stood in Sam Houston Park since 1972. Initially, it adorned the Scanlan family home on Main Street in Houston before being relocated to their residence in Arcola. The Fountain was later gifted to the Heritage Society, and its permanent place was found in the park.

The Fountain is an elegant structure made of green-painted cast iron, with a pool measuring 30 inches in height and the Fountain itself standing an impressive 12 feet tall. Its most recent restoration was completed in 1999.

The Fountain honors Thomas Scanlan, an influential figure in Houston's history. Born in County Limerick, Ireland, Scanlan immigrated to America as a child and arrived in Houston in 1853. He became a prosperous merchant and significant political leader during Reconstruction. Appointed alderman of the Third Ward by the Union government in 1868, Scanlan later served as Mayor of Houston in 1870, where his leadership oversaw significant infrastructure advancements in the city. Beyond politics, he held executive roles in several key companies, including the Houston City Street Railway Company, Houston Gas Light Company, and Houston Water Works Company. Scanlan passed away in 1906, leaving a lasting legacy.

J.L. Mott Iron Works, a renowned manufacturer of the time, crafted the Scanlan Fountain. Interestingly, it is believed that in 1917, artist Marcel Duchamp selected a urinal from J.L. Mott Iron Works' Manhattan showroom and reimagined it as the avant-garde artwork *Fountain*, exhibited at the Society of Independent Artists. This association adds a unique artistic connection to the history of the Scanlan Fountain.

Houston Cotton Exchange

Thomas William House Sr. was instrumental in founding the Houston Cotton Exchange in 1874. This establishment underscored his deep-rooted engagement in the cotton industry.

Supplemental Materials

Plates (maps, plats, and documents)

The following plates provide visual and documentary context for Arcola's land history, community development, and key institutions:

- Plate 1: Map—Abstracts 25 (David Fitzgerald), 31 (William Hall), 170 (Manuel Escalero), and 352 (I&GN Railroad) overlaid on modern Arcola (FM 521, Masterson, Highway 6).
- Plate 2: Facsimile—Excerpt from Sherman's Special Field Orders No. 15, illustrating the promise and limits of post-emancipation land redistribution.
- Plate 3: GLO Index Map—Manuel Escalero Survey (Abstract 170) and neighboring land grants in the Arcola area.
- Plate 4: Deed—1874 Phelps purchase of 3,129.25 acres, showing square vara totals and land transfer history.
- Plate 5: Plat—1935 Arcola Farms subdivision, with Jungman & Thompson survey notes.
- Plate 6: Plat—Minnequa Gardens (1950s), including Lot One callouts and 2021 legal notice.
- Plate 7: Church Record—1943 Palestine Baptist deed reference within the William Hall League, documenting Black community landholding.
- Plate 8: Railroad Timetable—1858 Houston Tap & Brazoria segment through Jonathan Waters' Arcola Plantation, showing early transportation routes.
- Plate 9: Freedmen's Bureau—Example labor contract from Fort Bend County, illustrating post-emancipation labor arrangements.

Timeline of land, law, and Arcola

Year	Event	Local resonance
1835–1839	Escalero's military service, capture, and escape	Basis for bounty/donation grants shaping Abstract 170
1858	Houston Tap & Brazoria line crosses Arcola Plantation	The rail corridor that future Arcola families follow
1865	Emancipation; Sherman's Orders No. 15	Promise of land, quickly revoked; Texas not included
1866	Black Codes in Texas; Southern Homestead Act (excludes TX)	Criminalization funnels labor; no public land access
1869	Arcola Post Office established at FM 521 & Masterson	Name and location fixed on federal maps
1870–1883	I&GN consolidation; Fifty Cent Act & repeal	Speculation and land sales reshape access
1870–1895	Palestine Baptist was founded; family land purchases in the Hall League	Civic anchor and land accumulation in Abstract 31
1874–1889	Phelps purchases and transfers Escalero lands	Consolidation into corporate portfolios
1935	Arcola Farms platted (290.25 acres)	Depression-era community mapping and growth
1950s–	Minnequa Gardens platted; Lot	Railroad land becomes homes; public record endures

253

Glossary of land and archival terms

- Abstract (Texas): County/GLO index identifier for original grants/surveys; not a unit of land.
- League and Labor: Texas land measures; one league ≈ 4,428.4 acres; one labor ≈ 177.14 acres.
- Vara: A linear measure of 33 1/3 inches; one acre ≈ 5,645.376 square varas.
- Bounty and Donation Grants: Land awards for military service (bounty) or special acts (donation).
- Freedom Colony: Independent Black settlement anchored by churches, schools, cemeteries, and mutual aid.
- Metes and Bounds: Boundary description using bearings, distances, and landmarks.
- Chain of Title: Sequence of historical transfers of a property.
- Plat: Official map of a subdivision with lots, streets, and easements.

Researcher and Descendant Toolkit

- Locating deeds and plats:
  - Fort Bend County Clerk: Deed Books A–Z; Plat Records (include book/page).
  - Texas General Land Office: Grant files, bounty/donation ledgers; Abstract index maps.
- Citing records:
  - Deed example: Fort Bend County, Deed Book X, p. ###, Grantor → Grantee, date (recorded date), legal description (Abstract ##, League, Lot).
  - Plat example: Fort Bend County Plat Records, Slide ##/Cabinet ##, *Arcola Farms*, filed date, surveyor.
- Oral history starters:
  - *Who first settled your family on this land? Where are their graves?*
  - *Which paths did your elders walk—river, rail, church, or fields?*
- Preservation steps:
  - Photograph headstones and deeds; geo-tag with GPS.
  - Record cemetery maps; file affidavits of heirship; back up to multiple repositories.

Acknowledgments

To the elders and descendants who carry Arcola's names; to the church mothers and deacons whose records outlived storms; to the county clerks, archivists, and mapmakers who kept the paper trail intact; and to those whose stories were nearly erased—this work is for and because of you.

References

1. Abraham Jones v. City of Arcola, Texas, Robert E. Hebert, Receiver for the City of Arcola, and City Council for the City of Arcola, No. 93CV1127 (S.D. Tex. 1993).
2. Acts of the Sixth Legislature of the State of Texas. (1866). *Black Codes*. Texas State Legislature.
3. AquaBest®. (2025, February 8). *Best multimedia carbon filtration system in Dubai*. https://aquabestksa.com/product/best-multi-media-carbon-filtration-system-in-dubai/
4. Archdiocese of Galveston–Houston Archives. (1937). *Estate correspondence of the Scanlan sisters*. Houston, TX.
5. Around the neighborhoods: The land called Sienna Plantation —I & —III. Bowden, C. V. (2015). *Fort Bend Independent*. www.fbindependent.com
6. Austin's Colony - Cradle of Texas Chapter #33 Sons of the American Revolution. (n.d.). https://cradletxsar.org/austins-colony/
7. Benham, P. (1995). *Houston politics during Reconstruction*. Houston: Rice University Press.
8. Billy Baines obituary. (2010). *Houston Chronicle*. https://www.legacy.com/us/obituaries/houstonchronicle/name/billy-baines-obituary?id=22922340
9. Bizapedia. *Leavings Concrete Company, Texas Domestic For-Profit Corporation filing*. Filed Dec. 29, 1977. File No. 0042328200. Registered agent: Donald R. Leavings.
10. Blackmon, D. A. (2008). *Slavery by another name: The re-enslavement of Black Americans from the Civil War to World War II*. New York: Anchor Books.
11. Bones, F. (1968). *The recollections of Button Fenn of Arcola*. Richmond: Fort Bend County Historical Commission.
12. Bowlin, C. M. (2017). Black landownership and the Texas Homestead Act. *Journal of Southern History, 83*(2), 325–354.
13. Broussard, Claude Joseph Jr. *Texas Certificate of Death*, State File No. 95600. Texas Department of Health, filed January 12, 1981.

14. Broussard, Claude J. Jr. "Broussard Services Held." *Fort Bend Mirror*, December 14, 1980. Obituary clipping.
15. FindUsLocal. *Leavings Concrete Co Inc.* Contractor listing. Services: patios, driveways, foundations, stamped concrete, concrete pavers.
16. Fort Bend County Historical Records. Cemetery designation for Claude J. Broussard Family Cemetery (FB-C046). Fort Bend County, Texas.
17. R.R. Bowker. *Who's Who in American Politics*, Sixth Edition, 1977–1978. New York: R.R. Bowker, 1977.
18. R.R. Bowker. *Who's Who in American Politics*, Seventh Edition, 1979–1980. New York: R.R. Bowker, 1979.
19. Burnham v. Arcola Sugar Mills Co., 2 F. Supp. 738 (S.D. Tex. 1932); *City officials face eviction. Paris News.* (1984, February 17).
20. Campbell, R. J. (1989). *Gone to Texas: A history of the Texas prison system.* Austin: Texas State Historical Association.
21. City of Houston. (1870). *Municipal records of mayoral appointments.* Houston, TX.
22. Collection: William Walter Phelps Papers. (n.d.). Archives and Special Collections, Rutgers University.
23. Congregation of Divine Providence Archives. (1937). *Letters of Stella Scanlan.* San Antonio, TX.
24. Corgan Architecture. (2024). *Design specifications: Middle School 16.* Dallas: Corgan Studio Archives.
25. Cultural resources assessment of the proposed Siena Plantation development. Espey, Huston & Associates, Inc. (1984, September).
26. Dallas Morning News. (1908, April 5). *Children incarcerated alongside hardened criminals.* Dallas, TX.
27. DePillis, L. (2016, July 28). Texas's sugar land prison cemetery reveals the dark history of convict leasing. *Houston Chronicle.* https://www.houstonchronicle.com

28. Eilers, A. (1968). Early schooling in Arcola. In Bones, F. *History of Fort Bend Schools*. Richmond: Fort Bend County Historical Commission.

29. Evans, M. A. (2025, February 20). *Oral history*. Harriett's History Box Oral Archive.

30. Evans, M. A. (2023). *Personal interview: Oaklane and Mustang School memories*. Harriett's History Box Oral Archive.

31. Exploros. (n.d.). *Spindletop and the oil industry*. https://www.exploros.com/Social-Studies/Texas-History-ms/Age-of-Oil/Spindletop-and-the-Oil-Industry

32. FBC150 House Plantation Cemetery. (n.d.). *Deed – Arcola Sugar Mills Company to Gulf, Colorado & Santa Fe Railroad Co.*

33. Fenn House. (n.d.). *The Portal to Texas History*. https://texashistory.unt.edu/ark:/67531/metapth610715/

34. Fenn, M. M. (2003). *Glimpses of our history*.

35. Ferguson, C. M. (ca. 1860–1906). Lucko, P. M. (2020, October 22). https://www.tshaonline.org/handbook/entries/ferguson-charles-m

36. Fort Bend County Appraisal District. (n.d.). Survey Abstracts and Plat Maps: Abstract 25.

37. Fort Bend County Clerk's Office. (1836–1950). *Deed Books A–Z; Plat records for Arcola Farms (1935) and Minnequa Gardens (1950s)*.

38. Fort Bend County Clerk's Office. (1899–1903). *School plot filings: Arcola Colored School near St. John Missionary Baptist, Abstract 170. School District Parcel Records*.

39. Fort Bend County Clerk's Office. (1905). *Oaklane School construction filing, Abstract 170. District Infrastructure Records*.

40. Fort Bend County Clerk's Office. (1907). *Arcola Plantation map. Survey and plat records for Arcola Plantation boundaries and land use*.

41. Fort Bend County Clerk's Office. (1907). *Mount Zion land deed, Abstract 31. Deed Book 12, Page 417*.

42. Fort Bend County Clerk's Office. (1909). *Map of Arcola Sugar Mills Co. Plantation. Survey and plat records for Arcola Sugar Mills Company holdings.*

43. Fort Bend County Clerk's Office. (1910). *Mustang School site filing, Abstract 170. School District Expansion Records.*

44. Fort Bend County Clerk's Office. (1928). *Land deed: Reverend Elijah Carter donation, Abstract 170. Deed Book 24, Page 198.*

45. Fort Bend County Clerk's Office. (1954, May 12). *Arcola Heights Addition Plat.*

46. Fort Bend County Clerk's Office. (1954, May 12). *Arcola Heights Plat.*

47. Fort Bend County Clerk's Office. (1955). *Stand Land Survey.*

48. Fort Bend County Clerk's Office. (1969, April 8). *Pinedale Manor Subdivision Plat.*

49. Fort Bend County Historical Commission. (1960–2020). *School district maps and trustee listings.* Richmond: County Archives.

50. Fort Bend County Historical Commission. (n.d.). Arcola Baptist Church Records.

51. Fort Bend County Historical Commission. (n.d.). Freedmen's Schools in Arcola, 1903 Enrollment Records.

52. Fort Bend County Historical Commission. (1996). *Preservation appeals for Arcola Plantation.* Richmond, TX.

53. Fort Bend County Superintendent. (1900–1969). *Annual school census and enrollment reports.* Richmond: County Education Office.

54. Fort Bend ISD. (1950–2023). *Zoning maps and transportation plans.*

55. Fort Bend ISD. (1950–2025). *Campus enrollment records: Oaklane, Rosenwald, M.R. Wood, Dulles, Hightower, Elkins, Ridge Point, Crawford.*

56. Fort Bend ISD. (1959). *Consolidation vote and campus transfer records.* Richmond: Arcola ISD to Fort Bend ISD transition filings.

57. Fort Bend ISD. (2018, 2025). *Board meeting minutes: Naming committee proceedings.*

58. Fort Bend ISD. (2023). *Bond allocation documents: Middle School 16.*

59. Fort Bend ISD. (2024–2026). *Sustainability and net-zero campus planning documents.*

60. Fort Bend ISD. (2025). *Naming committee submissions and review logs.*

61. Fort Bend County Road Records.
Designation of Broussard Lane, Arcola, Texas. County roadway naming records.

62. Galveston Daily News. (1892, March 24; 1910, November 26). *New picnic grounds; Arcola Plantation.*

63. Ghost Hunters. (n.d.). *Haunted Galveston Island, Texas.* http://www.galvestonghost.com/hitchcock.html

64. Graham, P. T. (2023). *Back stories of history featuring Freedmen's Town.*

65. Griffen, B. (1936). *Biography of convict leasing in Texas.* Unpublished manuscript, Texas State Library and Archives Commission.

66. Harris County Clerk. Marriage License: Claude Joseph Broussard Jr. and Ruth Faye Delaney, issued June 24, 1956.

67. Hiciano Ramos, M. G. (2020). Work–family conflict in low-income households. *CUNY Academic Works.* https://academicworks.cuny.edu/cgi/viewcontent.cgi?article=4831&context=gc_etds

68. Hopper, C. (1972, September 19). *Brazoria boom buds. Houston Post.*

69. Houston Chronicle. (1908, March 12). *Men worked to death in the cane fields.* Houston, TX.

70. Houston Chronicle. (n.d.). *Arcola elects its first Black female mayor.* https://www.chron.com/neighborhood/article/Arcola-elects-its-first-black-female-mayor-9316248.php?form=MG0AV3

71. Houston Post. (1904, November 25). *Funeral of John Rutherford Fenn.* Houston, TX.

72. Houston Chronicle. (n.d.). *Arcola elects its first Black female mayor.* https://www.chron.com/neighborhood/article/Arcola-elects-its-first-black-female-mayor-9316248.php?form=MG0AV3

73. Houston Post. (1904, November 25). *Funeral of John Rutherford Fenn.* Houston, TX.

74. Imperial Sugar Company Records. (1870s–1910s). *Convict leasing contracts and subleases.* Sugar Land, TX.

75. International & Great Northern Railroad. (1873). *Charter and annual reports.* Railroad Commission of Texas.

76. International – Great Northern Railroad Company bond certificate. (n.d.). *Ghosts of Wall Street.* https://ghostsofwallstreet.com/products/international-great-northern-railroad-company

77. International – Great Northern – Missouri Pacific Historical Society. (2025, January 26). https://mopac.org/mopac-history-post/international-great-northern/?form=MG0AV3

78. International Railroad bond certificate. (n.d.). *Ghosts of Wall Street.* https://ghostsofwallstreet.com/products/international-rail-road-company-texas

79. Jackson Street Hospital Campus – OakBend Medical Center. (2025, February 8). https://oakbendmedcenter.org/jackson-street-hospital-campus/?form=MG0AV3

80. Johnson, A. (1865, April 14). *Proclamation restoring confiscated lands.* National Archives.

81. Johnson Development. (2025, February 12). https://www.johnsondevelopment.com/mpc_sienna_plantation?form=MG0AV3

82. Oral Histories Project, Fort Bend County. (n.d.). Freedmen Families of Arcola…

83. Public address record. *2203 McKeever Road, Rosharon, TX 77583.* Last known business location.

84. Riceton–Arcola Cemetery Association. (n.d.). Burial Records and Headstone Transcriptions.

85. Klucker, A. (1922, September 4). *Photograph of Ku Klux Klan initiation near Richmond, TX.*

86. Land Grant. (n.d.). *Texas General Land Office.* https://www.glo.texas.gov/archives-heritage/search-our-collections/land-grant-search/land-grant/12404

87. Layne Christensen Co. (2009, October 5). Wastewater plant expansion enables economic development. *Wastewater Digest.* https://www.wwdmag.com/case-studies/article/10977187/layne-christensen-co-wastewater-plant-expansion-enables-economic-development

88. Lee, O. (n.d.). *Juneteenth: A children's story.* National Juneteenth Foundation. www.njof.org

89. Texas General Land Office. (n.d.). Survey Abstracts: Fort Bend County.

90. Life on the Brazos River – Sugar Land Railroad. (2025, January 26). http://lifeonthebrazosriver.com/Sugar%20Land%20Railroad.pdf

91. LM Inkley Company. (1957, February 9). *Owners and developers.*

92. Lonn, E. (1928). *Desertion during the Civil War.* Princeton University Press.

93. Manta. *Leavings Concrete Co.* Business profile. Established 1969. Owner: Donald Leavings. Employees: 2–4. Annual revenue: $100,001–$500,000.

94. McDavid, L. (2021, April 27). *First Ward, Houston.* Retrieved March 11, 2025, from https://www.tshaonline.org/handbook/entries/first-ward-houston?form=MG0AV3

95. Morales demand's Arcola's records. (1993, July 21). *Orange Leader,* p. 11.

96. Moorhead, G. (2017, April 17). *Report of opinion Scanlan House at Siena Plantation.*

97. Original plat for Arcola Farms. (n.d.). *Ash Avenue and Oak Avenue.*

98. Perkinson, R. (2010). *Texas tough: The rise of America's prison empire.* New York: Metropolitan Books.

99. Sarah Catherine Fitzgerald Fenn Cox. (n.d.). *Life on the Brazos River.*
http://lifeonthebrazosriver.com/SarahCatherineFitzgeraldFennCox.htm

100.   Scanlan Foundation History. (2016).

101.   Scanlan Foundation Acquisition Records. (post-1908). *Documentation of transfer and continuity of assets after sale.*

102.   Sherman, W. T. (1865, January 16). *Special Field Orders No. 15.* U.S. War Department.

103.   Smallwood, J. M. (2007). *Freedom colonies: Independent Black Texans in the time of Jim Crow.* University of Texas Press.

104.   Southern Homestead Act of 1866, ch. 64, 14 Stat. 66 (1866).

105.   Sowell, A. J. (1904). *History of Fort Bend County,* p. 88.

106.   Southwest Educational Project (SWEP). (2022). *HBCU tour documentation and board member profiles.* Houston: SWEP Publications.

107.   Stephen F. Austin | TSLAC. (n.d.).
https://www.tsl.texas.gov/treasures/giants/austin/austin-01.html

108.   Texans' struggle for freedom and equality exhibit – Anglo-American colonization efforts. (n.d.). *Texas State Library.*
https://www.tsl.texas.gov/lobbyexhibits/struggles-anglo

109.   Texas Education Agency. (1920–1930). *Biennial reports.* Austin: State Superintendent's Office.

110.   Texas General Land Office. (1850–1859). *Bounty warrant ledgers.* Texas GLO Archives.

111.   Texas General Land Office. (n.d.). *Abstracts 31, 171, and 352 — Survey boundaries and acreage confirmation for Arcola Plantation holdings.*

112.   Texas Historical Commission Atlas. (n.d.).
https://atlas.thc.texas.gov

113.   Texas Secretary of State Archives. (1903). *Charter filings for Arcola Sugar Mills Company, Inc.,* Austin, TX.

114. Texas Secretary of State Corporate Filings. (1899, 1903). *Incorporation charter and subsequent reorganization/recapitalization filings.*

115. Texas State Library and Archives Commission. (n.d.). *Convict leasing in Texas, 1867–1912.* Austin, TX: Author. https://www.tsl.texas.gov

116. Texas State Library and Archives Commission. (1909). Report of the House Committee on Penitentiaries. Austin, TX: State Printing Office.

117. Turner, M. A. (n.d.). *Sugar Land: The rise of a company town.*

118. United States Bureau of Refugees, Freedmen, and Abandoned Lands. (1865–1872). *Freedmen's Bureau records (Microfilm M1900).* National Archives.

119. United States Bureau of the Census. (1910). *Prisoners and juvenile delinquents in institutions, 1904.* Washington, DC: Government Printing Office.

120. United States Census Bureau. (1870–1970). *Federal census records: Fort Bend County, Texas.* Washington, DC: U.S. Government Printing Office.

121. United States Court of Appeals, Fifth Circuit. (1933, December 15). *Burnham v. Arcola Sugar Mills Company, Inc.* Case opinion.

122. U.S., Appointments of U.S. Postmasters, 1832–1971. (n.d.). *National Archives.*

123. Vollmar, J. (2010). *Railroads of Fort Bend County and Rosenberg Museum.* Arcadia Publishing.

124. Ward, D. C. (1971). The Convict Lease System in Texas, 1867–1912. *Southwestern Historical Quarterly, 75*(1), 1–25.

125. Waters, J. D. (1850s–1860s). Plantation Records, Arcola, Texas.

126. Watson, L. (2018). Hell hole on the Brazos: Convict leasing and the Imperial Sugar plantations. *Journal of Southern History, 84*(3), 555–590.

127. Weiskopf, D. L. (2009). *Rails around Houston.* Arcadia Publishing.

128. Yellow Pages. *Leavings Concrete Co Inc.* Listing at 2203 McKeever Road, Rosharon, TX 77583. Phone: (713) 851-4337. "Specializing in quality concrete projects for the last 45 years."

About the Author
Priscilla T Graham

Priscilla T Graham is a Gulf War veteran, documentary artist, genealogist, and cultural preservationist whose work is transforming how Black communities across Texas and the American South reclaim their histories. As a fifth-generation descendant of Harriett Mitchell of Thomas County, Georgia, Priscilla's dedication is rooted in lineage, memory, and the responsibility to protect stories nearly lost to time.

Her journey into preservation began with a personal calling to serve communities with excellence, dignity, and truth. For more than a decade, Priscilla has built one of the most extensive contemporary archives of Black heritage in Texas. Her documentation spans historic settlements, churches, cemeteries, neighborhoods, and community landmarks—capturing the lived experiences, ancestral ties, and cultural footprints that define these spaces. Through photography, filmmaking, research, oral history, and digitization, she preserves cultural landscapes that are often overlooked, endangered, or forgotten.

Priscilla is the author of an expansive catalog of historical and documentary works, including the *Hallowed Ground* series, *Freedmen's Town Legends*, *Freedmen's Town Then & Now*, *Texas 100 Year Old Churches*, and numerous books on Houston's historic Black neighborhoods. Her exhibitions have been featured at the Buffalo Soldiers National Museum, the Contemporary Arts Museum Houston,

Hogan Brown Gallery, and the Houston Freedmen's Town Conservancy.

Her newest work, ***The Back Stories of History: Featuring Arcola***, continues her mission by restoring the memory of a community whose history has long been overlooked. Through this book, she documents Arcola's families, churches, civic leaders, and cultural landscapes with the same care, accuracy, and reverence that define her preservation practice.

Priscilla's preservation work has earned recognition from civic leaders and institutions across Texas, including proclamations from the City of Houston and Fort Bend County. Most notably, she received a Congressional Resolution of Recognition from the 18th District of Texas, awarded by Congresswoman Sheila Jackson Lee for her photography featured in "Broken Promises, Seeking Reparations". Through her archival studio, Harriett's History Box, LLC, she continues to expand a growing body of work that safeguards Black and Indigenous histories for future generations.

Priscilla lives and works in Arcola, Texas, where she remains deeply committed to documenting, protecting, and uplifting the stories of the community she calls home. Her work ensures that Arcola's history— and the histories of countless other communities—will be remembered with dignity, accuracy, and honor.

www.ingramcontent.com/pod-product-compliance
Lightning Source LLC
Chambersburg PA
CBHW070119100426

42744CB00010B/1863